GET A RAISE IN 7 DAYS

Books and CD-ROMs by Drs. Ron and Caryl Krannich

GET A RAISE IN 7 DAYS
10 Salary Savvy Steps to Success

Ronald L. Krannich, Ph.D.
Caryl Rae Krannich, Ph.D.

IMPACT PUBLICATIONS
Manassas Park, VA

GET A RAISE IN 7 DAYS: 10 Salary Savvy Steps to Success

Liability/Warranty: The authors and publisher have made every attempt to provide the reader with accurate, timely, and useful information. However, given constant changes in the economy and variations from one employer to another, they make no claims that this information will remain accurate and useful at the time of reading. Furthermore, this information is presented for reference purposes only. The authors and publisher make no claims that using this information will guarantee the reader a raise or promotion. The authors and publisher shall not be liable for any loss or damages incurred in the process of following the advice presented in this book.

Library of Congress Cataloguing-in-Publication Data

Krannich, Ronald L.
    Get a raise in 7 days / 10 salary savvy steps to success / Ronald L. Krannich, Caryl Rae Krannich.
        p. cm.
    Includes bibliographical references and index.
    ISBN 1-57023-099-4
        1. Promotions. 2. Wages. 3. Career development. 4. Negotiation in business. I. Krannich, Caryl Rae. II. Title.
    HF5549.5.P7K7 1999
    650.14—dc21   98-40540
                                                                      CIP

Publisher: For information on Impact Publications, including current and forthcoming publications, authors, press kits, online bookstore, and submission requirements, visit Impact's Web site: *www.impactpublications.com*

Publicity/Rights: For information on publicity, author interviews, and subsidiary rights, contact the Public Relations Department: Tel. 703/361-7300.

Sales/Distribution: All bookstore sales are handled through Impact's trade distributor: National Book Network, 15200 NBN Way, Blue Ridge Summit, PA 17214, Tel. 1-800-462-6420. All other sales and distribution inquiries should be directed to the publisher: Sales Department, IMPACT PUBLICATIONS, 9104-N Manassas Drive, Manassas Park, VA 20111-5211, Tel. 703/361-7300, Fax 703/335-9486, or Email *raise@impactpublications.com*

Contents

CHAPTER 3: Test Your Salary I.Q. and Compensation Value 38

CHAPTER 4: Your Seven Day Success Plan 47

PART II

10 STEPS TO SALARY SUCCESS

CHAPTER 5: Analyze Your Situation 61

Chapter 10: Structure the Situation 133

Chapter 11: Develop A 3-Minute "Perfect Salary Pitch" 149

Chapter 12: Anticipate Objections To Your Pitch 160

Chapter 13: Close and Follow-Up With Impact 172

Responsibilities

The pages that follow are designed to provide you with useful information on how to best improve your compensation package with your current or future employer. Neither the publisher nor authors can guarantee your success in using this information and advice. Employers, circumstances, situations, and individual negotiating capabilities differ to the extent that results may vary considerably from one user to another.

When developing your own approach to getting a raise, keep in mind that you are dealing with a very delicate issue that can influence your long-term relationship with your boss. Indeed, if you don't handle this situation properly, you could damage your relationship with your employer as well as jeopardize your job. Be sensitive to this situation by focusing on what's really important to both you and your boss—added-value for performance.

In the end, it is your responsibility to know your boss and your situation. We outline the key ingredients that go into developing an effective strategy for getting a raise. It is up to you to analyze your situation, as well as your goals, and develop strategies that give you the best chance of a positive outcome.

Preface

W hy should I give you a raise? That's the key question you need to address when it's time to talk about a raise with your boss. How you answer that question will largely determine what your compensation package will look like in the future. Answer it right, and you'll likely walk away with a raise. Answer it wrong, and you may be shown the door. Whatever the outcome, your answer will most likely affect your future relationship with your employer.

Get a Raise in 7 Days grew out of our previous work with job seekers who used our popular companion volume, *Dynamite Salary Negotiations: Know What You're Worth and Get It!* (Impact Publications, 1998), a book that primarily focused on how to negotiate a salary with a new employer. By contrast, this book focuses specifically on how to improve one's compensation package once on the job. In fact, the major impetus for writing this book came from several television and radio shows and newspaper and magazine interviews we did on *Dynamite Salary Negotiations*.

While many questions we dealt with concerned the job seeker negotiating a compensation package with a new employer, the questions inevitably turned to the whole issue of how to talk about money to one's current boss.

Indeed, we discovered a tremendous need for this particular book. Few people feel comfortable "seeing the boss" about their paycheck or dealing with various elements in their compensation package. They often go into a salary review meeting unprepared and leave having accepted the boss's offer. Feeling uncomfortable talking about both themselves and the boss's money, most people feel this whole subject is really the dark side of employment—filled with secrets, inequities, distrust, and failed attempts to talk money to power. The more we got into the subject, the more we learned that talking money to power is really all about doing one's job beyond what is normally expected and communicating one's accomplishments and salary comparables to one's boss.

Get a Raise in 7 Days attempts to bring lots of sunshine to the whole subject of talking money to power. Our approach is that of a win-win outcome for both the employee and employer—mutual interests and shared benefits. Although we usually put ourselves in the shoes of the employee, at times we also "play boss" by telling employees what bosses really look for in subordinates.

If there was ever one on-the-job area where you need to demonstrate entrepreneurial skills, it is in talking to your boss about your compensation. Start by taking seven days to follow the ten steps outlined in the following chapters. If you do this, you should have an excellent chance of convincing your boss that you are worth more than what's reflected in your current compensation package. Like many other employees, you are probably under-compensated in your current position because you haven't paid much attention to your salary since you were hired. With *Get a Raise in 7 Days*, you should be able to take better care of your paycheck. At least this book should help you start in the right direction.

GET A RAISE IN 7 DAYS

1

The Truth About Job Money

Job money. It's usually good money, but it never seems to be good enough money. We all want more of it, sooner rather than later.

Job money is different from other types of money. Job money comes from the work you do for others—their money in exchange for your labor and talent. It's supposed to represent your performance and your value to an employer. But it often reflects many other considerations, some of which seem peripheral to your job performance—your salary history, your negotiating skills, and your position in relationship to other positions in an organization.

Talking Money to Power

If you're like millions of other people, your job money is your main source of income. It's also a significant indicator of your value to others and your sense of self-worth. And if you are like many others, your job money never seems to be enough. You have needs that often exceed your salaried income. You probably want more, or at least as much as you feel you should be getting for the type of work you do. So what do you do when your job money is not enough?

You probably want to, but most likely are reluctant to, say this to your boss:

"I would like to make more money in my current job because I need more money to get ahead in today's economy."

While this statement may reflect a self-centered attitude of need and greed, it's often true. You simply want to make more money doing what you do best and in a job you enjoy doing.

But here's the truth about job money—the financial rewards of your present job probably won't expand as rapidly as your income needs. In addition, once you're hired, chances are your salary will not keep pace with the salaries offered new hires. If you want to make sure you're being paid what you're really worth, you'll need to do something about this situation, such as quit your job for a higher paying one or talk to your boss about getting more money.

I'm Happy, But I Need More Money

So you think you're unpaid? Unappreciated? You really think you're worth more in today's job market? How much more?

So what are you going to do? Look for greener pastures? What about talking to your boss about a raise or promotion?

Regardless of what some employment pontificators say about high degrees of workforce unhappiness, surveys continue to point out that over 85% of workers are relatively satisfied with their current jobs, a figure that has not changed much over the past 30 years. While many people may dream of greener pastures, in reality they seem to be relatively content in their present jobs. Indeed, most people really are not interested in looking for another job or changing careers, especially when they learn the financial rewards are not significantly different from their present job. They are more interested in keeping their job and getting ahead on the job than in abandoning ship. When it comes to the money question, most of them would like to be better compensated in their current job.

> Surveys continue to point out that over 85% of workers are relatively satisfied with their current jobs.

What they, and probably you, really need to do is talk money to power—have a serious conversation about money with your boss. How does your compensation compare to that of others in comparable positions within and outside your organization? But before talking money to power, ask yourself these basic "see the boss" questions:

- Are you prepared to initiate a serious salary discussion with your boss?

- When is the best time of day or week to meet?

- Who should set the time and place for the meeting?

- How do you open and close the conversation?

- Should you talk about a raise, promotion, bonus, and/or additional benefits?

- What's the best way to raise the money question and ask for more?

- What, if any, materials should you bring to the meeting?

- How can you best handle objections to your request?

Or are you like millions of others who are reluctant to "see the boss" about your financial future?

But maybe you're one of those people who would rather be told what the boss will give you rather than participate in a process that determines what you will be getting. If so, you probably deserve what you get because you're not prepared to talk money to power.

Keeping Score

Let's face it. Money is important to most people, especially when it comes to their job. Even for those who have more money than they know what to do with, money is one of the best indicators of their worth in comparison to others. It tells them where they stand in relationship to others. It also indicates "how I'm doing" in reference to themselves and their past compensation. In other words, money is a great scorekeeper—your salary indicates what you are really worth to others and it affects how you feel about yourself.

The following pages are all about playing the game, keeping score, and communicating your score to power. If you've decided to jump ship for greener pastures, see our companion volume on how to negotiate a salary with a new employer—*Dynamite Salary Negotiations*. By contrast, this particular book is designed to help you get ahead financially in your current job by making sure your boss rewards you properly. You want your boss to acknowledge, whether it's in the form of a salary increment, bonus, or promotion, that you should receive the highest compensation possible for your level of position and performance.

The 7-Day More Money Journey

Yes, it should only take seven days to get a raise, bonus, or promotion if you follow much of the advice outlined in this book. We offer no special tricks or "winning strategies" for doing so. Instead, we outline a clear *process*, which we call "steps," that should lead to salary success. Followed in sequence and implemented over a seven-day period, each step should lead to your desired goal—a raise, promotion, and/or bonus. By following our steps, you should avoid the many mistakes other people make. You'll learn how to best structure the situation, develop a 3-minute "Perfect Salary Pitch," anticipate and overcome objections to your salary request, close the deal, and go on to impress your boss with a record of accomplishments. In the end, you'll learn how important it is to "see the boss" and "talk money to power" in order to get a raise at any time.

What Do I Say, When?

Mixing sound strategies with sample dialogues, the following pages should give you a sense of "what it's really like" talking about money with your boss. Remember, this is not your typical meeting with your boss who usually talks about goals and targets, company strategies, team efforts, trouble shooting, and beating the competition. This is a meeting about how your talent can be best rewarded in a company of other talented individuals who also seek to be best rewarded. If you seek salary equity, or try to rise above the crowd, you may experience resistance to your efforts. At times, you may encounter a real life zero-sum game—giving more to you means giving less to others. At other times, you may be surprised to discover that your boss gives you what you want without any questions asked—so perhaps you should have asked for more!

And at other times, you may be shocked to discover that your salary initiative results in being shown the door—your boss really wanted to fire you but you've now self-destructed by demanding more money (saying "no" to you and accepting your resignation beats paying unemployment compensation attendant with firing you!). In other words, while the process of getting a raise may appear relatively clear-cut, the outcomes are anything but certain.

> **Talking money to power is one of the most important conversations you will ever undertake.**

The best advice we can give is to follow our 10-step plan which includes knowing your company and your boss.

Anticipating different types of salary scenarios, we've attempted to incorporate sound principles of persuasive communication in one-on-one settings with those who have the power to hire, fire, and reward employees. In the end, this book is all about talking money to power, one of the most important conversations you will ever undertake. Conquer this type of conversation, and you may well be on the road to greater career success.

Choose the Right Resources

We wish you well as you deal with your current compensation situation. Hopefully, the outcomes of your "meeting with the boss" will be positive for both you and your employer. However, if this is not the case and consequently you decide it's really time to start looking for greener and more lucrative pastures, you may want to review several of our job search books: *Change Your Job Change Your Life, Discover the Best Jobs For You, High Impact Resumes and Letters, Dynamite Resumes, Dynamite Cover Letters, Dynamite Tele-Search, 201 Dynamite Job Search Letters, Interview For*

Success, 101 Dynamite Answers to Interview Questions, Dynamite Networking For Dynamite Jobs, and *Dynamite Salary Negotiations*. We also address particular jobs and career fields in the following books: *The Complete Guide to Public Employment, The Directory of Federal Jobs and Employers, Find a Federal Job Fast, The Complete Guide to International Jobs and Careers, International Jobs Directory, The Educators Guide to Alternative Jobs and Careers,* and *Jobs For People Who Love Travel.* Many of these books are available in your local library and bookstore or they can be ordered directly from Impact Publications (see the "Career Resources" sections at the end of this book). Most of these resources, along with hundreds of others, are available through Impact's comprehensive online "Career Superstore":

www.impactpublications.com

Impact's site also includes new titles, specials, and job search tips for keeping you in touch with the latest in career information and resources. If you don't have access to the Internet, you can request a free copy of their career brochure by sending a self-addressed stamped envelope (#10 business size) and it will be mailed to you:

IMPACT PUBLICATIONS
ATTN: Free Career Brochure
9104-N Manassas Drive
Manassas Park, VA 20111-5211

Empower Yourself

The chapters that follow are all about empowerment—you have within you the power to shape your own destiny. Empowerment also should encompass dealing with the issue of on-the-job compensation. Indeed, if you follow our advice in the next three chapters of Part I ("Take Me to the Top"), you should be well oriented to the issue of compensation in today's new workplace. You'll develop a seven-day action plan that follows our ten steps to salary success in Part II. Each step constitutes a set of actions you should take to ensure the best possible outcomes for getting a raise in seven days.

As we stress throughout this book, getting a raise should come naturally to those who continually demonstrate their value to employers. The ability to communicate your value and translate it into monetary terms is what *Get a Raise in 7 Days* is all about. If you go to work each day without such a sense of value, you may be setting yourself up for future disappointments when it comes time to talk money to power.

Part I

Take Me To The Top

2

Welcome to the New World of Work

If you haven't noticed lately, you work in a very different work world from that of ten or twenty years ago. Within the past five years, millions of jobs have disappeared while millions of other jobs have been created. Skills you once used in abundance have probably become obsolete or have been transformed by new computer-driven technology. In the past few years, you've most likely acquired new skills in order to get ahead and/or function more effectively in your career or on various jobs you've held. While you may feel secure in your present job, chances are the job you have today may disappear tomorrow due to downsizing, or you may soon leave it for more rewarding opportunities.

You May Be Worth More Now

Compensation options also have changed considerably in the past decade. Indeed, there's more to compensation than just a gross salary figure. Bonuses, stock options, 401(k) plans, reimbursement accounts, incentivized pay systems, and flex-time are important issues that have enriched the language of compensation during the past decade. But the really good news for highly skilled employees is that they work in a talent-driven economy that is especially compensation-friendly. If you have the right mix of skills and experience in today's full employment, boom economy, you may be worth a lot more than your current salary. Consequently, it may be time for you to "see the boss" to talk about your total compensation package. Best of all, you may be the perfect candidate for getting a raise in seven days. Or, if seeing the boss doesn't result in expected outcomes, you may want to consider heading for greener pastures by negotiating a new salary with a new employer.

> **Today's highly skilled employees work in a talent-driven economy that is especially compensation-friendly.**

Compensation Myths and Realities

Numerous myths continue to influence the compensation many people receive. Several of these myths tend to work against people's best interests. Let's examine a few of the most important myths, and corresponding realities, that could influence your on-the-job income.

MYTH #1:   **Money will not make you happy; it's best to pursue non-monetary goals and values that will most likely make you and those around you happy.**

REALITY: Neither will poverty make you happy. Unless you don't know how to spend it, money can bring you and those around you great happiness. This "happiness argument" is a good rationalization for not doing as well financially as one could or should; it's an excuse for low achievement. And you will be especially unhappy when you learn you are being paid less than you're worth or receive less than others in the organization with comparable experience. There's a lot of truth to the old saying that *"Those who think money can't bring happiness don't know where to shop!"* You'll be especially happy when you get a salary commensurate with your value. While money may not make you happy, it makes life much more *convenient.* Better yet, it helps you *keep score* on your level of success in the world of work. The higher your salary, the more value you have to the employer and the better your score. Don't undersell yourself because of some old beliefs about the role of money in life. It's okay for talented people to make lots of money, constantly score high, and live a convenient and comfortable lifestyle. They are of great value to employers.

MYTH #2: **Compensation is largely determined by the employer. There's little I can do to influence what the employer gives me.**

REALITY: While employers may appear to be in control of compensation, they also function within a competitive employment arena, a market place that largely determines the value of positions. As an

employee, you should (1) know how other employers compensate individuals performing comparable functions in similar positions; (2) know
your comparative value; and (3) negotiate the best
deal possible with your employer. Armed with
solid knowledge of what other employers pay for
comparable work, you should be in a strong
position to negotiate a very good compensation
package.

MYTH #3: **Once I accept a job, I'm largely locked into the
salary and benefits I agreed upon. I'll have to
change employers in order to realize a significant increase in compensation.**

REALITY: Unless you really hate your job and employer, you
first need to "see the boss" before looking for
another employer whom you hope will compensate you better. It's not only wise on
your part to do this, it's also the
thoughtful and professional thing to
do with your current boss. Moreover,
the grass is not always greener on the
other side. Remember, it costs an
employer a lot to replace an employee. Indeed, some studies show
that it costs between $10,000 and
$20,000 to replace most employees. Many em-
ployers know it's cheaper in both the short- and
long-run to deal with the issue of compensation
fairly and equitably, especially if they know you
are a very valuable employee.

> You should first "see the
> boss" before looking for
> another employer whom
> you hope will compensate
> you better.

MYTH #4: **Employers try to pay the least amount possible; they are not anxious to provide additional benefits.**

REALITY: Only foolish employers engage in such predatory behavior. Like living with an abusive spouse, you should not be attracted to such negative characters. What most employers really want is good value in exchange for fair compensation. While some employers are *"penny wise but pound foolish"* by trying to hire the cheapest labor possible, in the long run they pay dearly for such meagerness with high turnover rates and unhappy employees. Smart employers will pay what is necessary, i.e., market value, to get the talent they need to run a sound and prosperous business. Be sure you're working for a smart employer who knows your value and the importance of compensation.

MYTH #5: **Compensation is the most important element in any job.**

REALITY: While important, compensation usually ranks third or fourth in most lists of what motivates employees at work. Most individuals want to be compensated equitably. The great motivators at work tend to be the (1) nature of the work itself, (2) the recognition one receives for a job well done, and (3) the degree of participation in the decision-making process. Compensation is something that needs to be dealt with in a timely and equitable manner.

MYTH #6:   **I should concentrate on the gross salary figure rather than on benefits when discussing my compensation package.**

REALITY: Yes and no, depending on the particular employer. According to U.S. Department of Labor studies, 44 percent of total compensation for the average worker comes in forms other than base salary. While social security makes up the largest portion of "benefits," numerous other benefits can make a significant difference in one's total compensation package. For example, if an employer offers stock options and you know you are with a growing company, the value of your stock could actually exceed your annual salary. Be sure to value all of your benefits and include them in a "total compensation figure." In the case of many small businesses that offer few benefits, you may want to concentrate on the salary figure. However, the trend amongst most employers in a boom economy is to offer more and more benefits as well as incentivize pay in order to both attract and retain top talent. Many employers may have more flexibility in increasing benefits than in raising base salaries. When considering benefits, follow this checklist:

> **44 percent of total compensation for the average worker comes in forms other than base salary.**

- ❏   Bonuses
- ❏   Commissions
- ❏   Overtime
- ❏   Reimbursement accounts

❑ Insurance (medical, dental, life, disability)
❑ 401(k) Plan
❑ Simplified Employee Pension (SEP)
❑ Pension/annuity
❑ Profit sharing
❑ Stock options
❑ Vacation days
❑ Personal leave days
❑ Flex-time
❑ Child care
❑ Tuition reimbursement
❑ Training opportunities
❑ Free parking
❑ Discounts
❑ Frequent flier miles

Taken together, many of these benefits can add substantially to the value of one's total compensation package, and especially if they are tax-free or tax-deferred benefits. Indeed, a $60,000 salary with one employer may be worth $75,000 with benefits, whereas another employer's $60,000 salary may be worth over $100,000 with benefits. If you add incentivized pay provisions, total compensation could be considerably more.

MYTH #7: **I'm probably paid less than other people here who have fewer responsibilities and don't work as hard as I do.**

REALITY: This old *"I'm better than they are and paid less, too"* attitude is typical for many employees who are probably unhappy with their current jobs.

Chances are that you are being paid "about right" for your level of responsibilities and work load. If you don't believe so, start job hunting to find out what your real market value is in the eyes of other employers. If you're unhappy with your present job, try to find out what you need to do to make it more rewarding other than increase your compensation. If you're really doing what you enjoy doing, your performance and joy will most likely be reflected in your paycheck. If not, it's time to "see the boss" about quantifying and better rewarding your value to the company.

MYTH #8: **Most employers have little flexibility when it comes to compensation. Company policies tend to dictate what all employees will get.**

REALITY: It depends on the company and particular positions. Most companies have little flexibility with entry-level positions and few negotiate much with inexperienced

> **Most companies have greater compensation flexibility with higher-level positions, and especially with executives.**

new hires. They have more flexibility with higher-level positions, and especially with executives. As you acquire more experience and advance to higher-level technical and/or professional positions, chances are you will discover employers are more and more willing to negotiate salaries and benefits as well as work out creative incentivized compensation plans. These are considered value-added positions that require flexible personnel and compensation policies to both attract and retain top talent.

MYTH #9: **Most employers really don't want to talk about compensation**.

REALITY: Most employers are concerned about productivity and performance. These are the same issues that lie at the heart of compensation. Indeed, this is the reason why many companies tie their performance appraisals to annual salary reviews. Employers want to know what it is you are doing to contribute to the well being of the organization. If you are making a definite contribution, most employers are more than willing to recognize such contributions with increased compensation.

MYTH #10: **My current compensation reflects what I'm really worth**.

REALITY: Your current compensation probably reflects a number of factors, few of which relate to your real worth: your negotiation skills; company policies; the industry you work in; and your geographic location and cost of living. The issue of your worth is one that relates to compensation comparables and your ability to communicate your performance to the employer.

MYTH #11: **It's okay to job-hop in today's economy; everyone is doing it, company loyalty is no longer**

important, and if I change jobs frequently, I'll look like I'm "in demand."

REALITY: There's not as much job-hopping going on as many people think or as many so-called employment experts say is taking place in today's overly-hyped new economy. Job security has remained remarkably stable for more than a decade. In fact, recent studies show that most people are relatively happy in their current jobs; most prefer staying where they are; and the amount of job-hopping has not increased significantly during the past 20 years. In fact, the Bureau of Labor Statistics finds that between 1983 and 1996, work tenure actually increased from 3.5 years to 3.8 years. Even during the so-called downsizing era of the 1990s, median job tenure rose from 3.6 years to 3.8 years. The sharpest declines in job tenure have been with males between the ages of 55 and 65. Not surprising, job tenure may actually increase during booming economic times as more and more employers create attractive forms of "job lock"— share their good fortunes with their employees in the form of bonuses, stock options, and other incentives. While changing jobs frequently may make you feel you're getting ahead in your career, in the eyes of most employers you are an unstable individual who will probably not say around long. If you leave within a year or two, your costs to the employers will be very high. Few employers are

> **Job-hopping has not increased at all during the past 20 years. Between 1983 and 1996, work tenure actually increased from 3.5 years to 3.8 years.**

in the business of training individuals who are always looking down the road for another employer. Despite what you may hear about loyalty to a company, employers still appreciate loyal employees.

MYTH #12: **The best way to get a raise is to threaten to quit, unless you get what you want.**

REALITY: Like any strategy, this one works in some cases. But it also can be very damaging to your continuing relationship with the employer, whether you stay or not. In fact, one of the quickest ways to be shown the door is to engage in idle threats about quitting. If you choose to use this strategy, be prepared to follow-through by making an exit if your demands are not met. Don't be surprised to discover, to your dismay, that you are not as valuable to the employer as you may think. Remember, two can play this game. While you may feel you are irreplaceable, in the eyes of most employers, everyone is replaceable. That's what *positions* are all about—they get filled with people who have the skills and abilities to perform specific tasks. As soon as you confuse yourself with the position, you may be on the road to a fast exit. In the end, you really are replaceable, just like everyone else in the organization.

MYTH #13: **The best way to get a raise is to prepare a list of reasons why you need more money and go through each reason with your boss.**

REALITY: Many people make the fatal mistake of communicating their financial needs to employers rather than stressing what it is they have been and will be doing for the employer. In other words, their rationale for getting a raise is self-centered rather than employer-centered; they approach the employer from a perspective of need and greed rather than stress their present and future performance. Your employer is not interested in your financial needs. For example, if you bought a new house or need to finance a car, or if you have new day care expenses attendant with the birth of a child, those are your personal problems. Don't burden your employer with such problems. If you do, you may appear financially irresponsible—taking on new expenses you really can't afford. While some employers may give you personal financial advice or counseling, few feel obligated to give you a raise because you decided to increase your standard of living by taking on new expenses! When you talk money to power, always do so from the perspective of power—what additional value will you give your boss if he or she gives you a raise?

MYTH #14: **Raises and promotions are two different issues that should be dealt with in separate meetings.**

REALITY: Raises and promotions should be dealt with at the same time. In many cases, a raise may be contingent upon being promoted to a higher level position that involves greater responsibilities. In fact, one effective strategy for getting a raise involves focusing on the question of promotion. Most individuals are hired to fill a particular position which has well defined duties and responsibilities. But after several months, perhaps unknown to your boss, the nature of the job changes substantially. Within a year or two the on-going duties and responsibilities of the position may have little resemblance to the original position description. In fact, you may be doing the work of another position altogether. If you do a thorough analysis of your current work, you too may discover that you are being paid for a position you no longer occupy. This may be the time to talk to your boss about redefining the position and adjusting your compensation accordingly. The outcome of doing so may be to create a new position or to be promoted to another position. Whatever the case, the justification for giving you a raise may be this type of promotion. Our advice: when preparing to "see the boss" about a raise, consider whether to ask for a promotion that involves increased compensation attendant with newly acquired responsibilities.

MYTH #15: **Individuals in performance-oriented sales and marketing positions are best able to negotiate a raise.**

REALITY: While individuals in such positions can easily identify performance indicators, such as monthly sales figures and market shares (*"increased sales 23% or $250,000 for the quarter"*), individuals in other positions also can and should develop performance indicators that go beyond mere workload statistics. If, for example, you are in an administrative support position, a good performance indicator might be the amount of money you saved the company by instituting new purchasing procedures (*"cut printing costs by 32% by instituting new bidding procedure"*). Anything you do to directly or indirectly save the company money, increase its profitability, or improve its market position should be included in your "performance portfolio"—your file of accomplishments to be communicated to your boss. Always think about identifying specific *indicators* that best represent your *achievements*. Without such indicators, you will be in a weak position to discuss and quantify why you deserve a raise.

> Develop a "performance portfolio"—your file of accomplishments to be communicated to your boss. Be sure to identify specific *indicators* that best represent your *achievements*.

Assume it is your responsibility to identify these indicators and tell your stories of accomplishments to your boss.

MYTH #16: **Once I'm hired, there's little I can negotiate other than my annual gross salary figure.**

REALITY: Depends on the organization. Many companies give employees equity in the form of stock or stock options after being with the company a few years. Companies strapped for cash, for example, may be willing to give you a greater share of equity in the company rather than a significant raise in base pay. Depending on the future outlook of the company, you may want to trade a greater share of equity for a salary raise. Many employees of start-up companies and executives in major corporations who took equity in the form of stock or stock options in exchange for a lower starting salary can testify to the wisdom of investing in the future of the company. Indeed, many have become very wealthy as the value of their company increased.

MYTH #17: **The best way to find out what I'm really worth is to ask others at work what they're making.**

REALITY: Now that's a great formula for getting fired! In fact, many employers have strict rules about discussing salaries. In many companies, one of the grounds for getting fired is discussing your salary with your co-workers. If you really want to find out what you're worth, do research with other employers in order to find out what they are paying for comparable positions. This research will result in establishing your fair "market value" which is what you are really worth in today's job market. If you compare your salary with others you work with, you may be comparing apples to oranges—positions, responsibilities, and functions may not be comparable.

MYTH #18: **I can expect my salary to increase each year by at least 4 percent—and more if I really impress my boss.**

REALITY: Yes, if you are willing to assume a continuing future economic boom and income-healthy employers. During the past few years, salaries increased at an average rate of 4.5 percent in an economy experiencing an annual inflation rate of 1.5 percent. Consequently, salaries were definitely on the increase, outstripping inflation by 3 to 1. However, one should not expect such increases to continue in the long-term. The full employment economy of 1997 and 1998 saw increased pressure on salaries because of labor shortages. But the pressure primarily took place at the recruitment stage. Employers tend to favor increasing benefits and other forms of compensation, such as performance bonuses and stock options, over increasing base salary. Also, don't expect the boom-boom economy to continue forever. Regardless of trendy new economic boom theories for decades ahead, chances are the boom bubble will eventually burst. Even if it doesn't, many companies that currently look very dynamic and profitable may quickly experience downturns, downsize, or even go bankrupt in what is a volatile boom economy. And within individual companies, upward pressures on salaries may only relate to a few high-demand positions. Millions of young people who first entered the job market during the booming 90's and subsequently saw their salaries and benefits steadily increase are not prepared for the sober employment and compensation difficulties that inevitably come with hard economic times. If and when the economy turns down, so may many salaries.

MYTH #19: You can negotiate anything as long as you know how to negotiate.

REALITY: Negotiation skills are especially useful in certain situations, such as when buying real estate, a car, or other high ticket items. Such skills work best when all players are willing and able to negotiate. Many job situations are open to negotiations, depending on the position and employer. Incentivized pay schemes appear to be very negotiable these days because they represent perfect win-win scenarios focusing on productivity and performance. However, many other job situations may be non-negotiable. Budgetary constraints and company compensation policies may limit the degree to which you can negotiate a raise or promotion with your boss.

> Incentivized pay schemes appear to be very negotiable these days because they represent perfect win-win scenarios focusing on productivity and performance.

MYTH #20: The boss has the power to give raises and promotions.

REALITY: Maybe, maybe not. In many cases your boss will need to see his or her boss before making any final decisions concerning raises and promotions. Consequently, you may need to wait a few days after your meeting with the boss before learning the status of your request for a raise or promotion.

Swimming in a Full-Employment Economy

Today's talent-driven economy has dramatically transformed the work place. Boasting an unemployment rate of 4.5 percent, jobs in this economy are plentiful for those who have the right skills and know where to find the jobs. Indeed, the roaring economy of 1998 was the best in over 30 years. It even led some observers to forecast a coming century marked by an unprecedented worldwide economic boom (see Knight Kiplinger, *World Boom Ahead*, and Harry S. Dent, Jr., *Roaring 2000's*). Gone were the boom and bust cycles of the 20th century accented by depressions, recessions, and Third and Fourth World poverty. Somewhere between 1990 and 1997 the old economy of the 20th century was transformed into a new 21st century economy driven by technology and the emergence of a huge worldwide middle class. Indeed, the year 1998 was merely a precursor to a new millennium marked by incredible economic growth. If this optimistic scenario plays out according to predictions, such a prosperous global economy would generate a tremendous number of new jobs. Full employment, rather than fluctuating unemployment rates, would characterize such a new economy. Since much of the boom would be driven by high technology, the demand for workers with high-tech skills would be great.

What happens to salaries and benefits in such an economy? Compensation issues should be in the forefront of this new world economy where skilled labor needs out-strip the availability of talented workers. In a competitive environment where talent is the main currency, employers will need to minimize worker turnover by offering more and more competitive salaries and benefits. Accordingly, rising wages should characterize this era of growth and prosperity.

A Talent-Driven Economy of "Haves" and "Have-Nots"

Regardless of what scenario plays out in the coming decade or century, the U.S. economy has increasingly become a talent-driven economy. Largely stimulated by new technology, the continuing growth of this economy requires the constant training and retraining of its workforce and the continuing expansion of a worldwide middle class that behaves like American middle-class consumers—high consumption and low savings. In this economy, skills quickly become obsolete and must be replaced by newer skills. Wage earners can expect to receive increased compensation in direct relationship to their ability to acquire and utilize newer skills sets.

The downside of this economy is its emerging class structure based upon specific workplace skills: the skilled "haves" and the less skilled "have-nots." Younger and more recently trained individuals tend to be the "haves"; older workers and those less trainable in new technologies tend to be the "have-nots." Compensation trends tend to favor the "haves" over the "have-nots." If you are over 40 years old, you may be endangered by becoming part of the "have-nots." You may see your wages erode, and getting a raise in seven days may be beyond your ability if you lack sufficient leverage to negotiate better compensation.

13 Compensation Trends That May Affect You

You should be aware of thirteen compensation trends that will most likely affect your ability to negotiate a raise in seven days. The most important ones include the following:

1. **Employers are more willing to negotiate salary and benefits in a tight labor market:** As long as unemploy-

ment remains under 6 percent and many jobs remain un-
filled, employers know they are in a seller's market and
thus need to offer more competitive compensation packages
to both attract and retain top talent. To lose important talent
in such a job market can be very costly to a company that
must recruit and train new employees. The loss of such
employees also means lost opportunity costs for a company.

> **In a highly competitive economy, lost opportunity costs for a company will be higher than their recruitment and training costs.**

In a highly competitive economy,
lost opportunity costs for a company will be higher than their
recruitment and training costs. Assuming you are a talented and
highly desirable employee, chances
are your employer will be receptive
to discussing compensation at any
time.

2. **Retention of a quality workforce becomes an increasingly important issue in company compensation policies.**
   Forget all those trendy "end of company loyalty" and "job-
   hopping" theories. Employers increasingly recognize that
   companies with a competitive advantage are those that are
   able to recruit and retain top talent. They also recognize the
   fact that most talented employees enjoy working for employers who offer important tangible and intangible benefits, such as:

   A. A workplace culture that enables them to grow
      professionally.

   B. Continuous recognition and appreciation of their
      accomplishments—they feel needed and wanted.

    C. Competitive compensation that reflects their real
       value to the company.

Any company that experiences an annual turnover rate of 20 percent or more is at a competitive disadvantage in today's economy. Their recruitment and training costs will be extraordinarily high in comparison to competitors who may have very high retention rates. The goal of many employers will be to keep the turnover rate under 5 percent. Consequently, employee loyalty and retention will become more important issues for employers who must increasingly adjust company compensation policies to retain talented employees in a tight labor market.

3. **Compensation will take on increasingly diverse and attractive forms.** More and more employees are looking for a diverse mix of attractive benefits in addition to a decent base salary. These benefits include disability insurance, 401(k) plans, reimbursement accounts, and flex-time. Because most such benefits are in the form of tax-free or tax-deferred compensation, they look increasingly attractive to employees. For example, $20,000 in employer-provided benefits can translate into the equivalent of $30,000 in additional income, since you would have to purchase those benefits with after tax dollars. The most competitive companies will offer stock options that have the potential of spreading new wealth to employees. Stock options not only hold the promise of generating new wealth amongst those who contribute to the increased growth and prosperity of the company, they create a new sense of identity and loyalty amongst employees who have an important stake in making the company successful.

4. **Individuals in high-level professional and technical positions will have an easier time getting raises than employees in other positions:** In most organizations, the highest salaries tend to go to those who generate the greatest value or contribute the most to the bottomline. Such employees are in a better position to negotiate their salaries and request additional benefits because they cost the most to replace in terms of both training and opportunity costs. Individuals occupying entry-level or low-demand positions will be in the weakest position to ask for a substantial raise and get it.

5. **Base salaries will tend to increase incrementally once you've accepted a job.** Don't expect employers to give substantial annual raises beyond a standard 2-5 percent across-the-board annual increment. While such raises may not reflect one's productivity and true value to an organization, from the perspective of the employer, they tend to be equitable and thus expeditious for the group as a whole.

6. **Child care benefits will play an increasingly important role in employee compensation packages.** More and more employees will seek out employers who offer either on-site or backup (emergency) child care services. Given the rising costs of child care services for two-career families and the increasing difficulties in finding good, dependable, and convenient child care services, many employers understand it's good personnel policy to offer on-site or backup child care services to both attract and retain talented employees. In fact, many individuals today will not consider working for an employer unless they offer at least some backup child care services. In 1998 approximately 13 percent of all

employers offered such services, and the numbers were expected to significantly increase in the coming decade. More and more employers will discover it makes good economic sense to become very family-friendly.

7. **Employers will increasingly offer a variety of benefits that translate into significant salary raises for employees.** Employers will increasingly understand the important role benefits can play in compensation packages. Giving benefits in lieu of a cash raise can be a win-win situation for both the employer and employee. Employers save by not having to pay additional social security taxes on a base salary increase or have their unemployment compensation rates increase. Employees come out ahead when they receive benefits that constitute tax-free or tax-deferred forms of compensation. For example, an employee receiving a $2,000 raise may only receive $1,400 in real, after-tax income. If the same $2,000 were given as tax-free or tax-deferred benefits (life insurance, child care, or employer contributions to a 401[k] plan), the benefit may be worth $2,800 in real income, or twice as much as a cash raise. As more and more employers and employees understand the real economics of benefits versus cash, compensation packages should take different forms other than a straight cash raise. It will be to everyone's advantage to increasingly focus on tax-free and tax-deferred benefits in lieu of cash.

> It will be to everyone's advantage to increasingly focus on tax-free and tax-deferred benefits in lieu of cash.

8. **Employees who think in terms of "incentivizing" their positions are more likely to get higher raises and em-**

ployer compliance than those who only focus on a specific percentage increase or dollar raise. When you "see the boss" about a raise, make sure you answer the most important question on the mind of the employer—*"Why should I give you X (your requested raise) rather than Y (my proposed raise)?"* You need to come up with concrete reasons that support your request. One of the best ways to bridge the gap between X and Y is to talk about incentivizing your pay. For example, try proposing a special bonus, which may be based on a percentage of your current salary, if you achieve certain performance goals that exceed your current performance. This may be an offer your employer cannot refuse because you will more than justify your bonus by adding greater value to the organization. Indeed, one of the hottest trends in compensation today is to incentivize pay by linking it to specific, quantifiable performance.

9. **Sharing salary information with fellow employees will remain serious grounds for dismissal.** Salary information in most organizations is supposed to be a tightly held management secret. Few things are more disruptive to an organization than when employees discover what others in the organization make, what raises they received, or how well they negotiated with the boss. In many companies such a breach of confidentiality is grounds for immediate dismissal. Since salary differences inevitably raise questions about equity, knowledge of these differences amongst employees tends to erode organizational morale. If you're interested in knowing how your salary compares to others, do your salary research with employees in comparable positions in other organizations. Such research will help establish your "market value" as well as provide you with

important data to establish your salary credibility. If you reveal to management that you've been doing "salary research" within your company, you may be quickly shown the unemployment door for engaging in potentially disruptive behavior that could seriously threaten organizational cohesion.

10. **Useful salary and benefit information will be more easily accessible to everyone.** While salary and benefit information used to be one of best kept corporate secrets and many employees remain in the dark concerning their market value, today this information is widely disseminated through numerous salary studies that can be easily found in most public libraries as well as on the Internet. Several Web sites also include "salary calculators" that enable users to figure out their salary needs. This information should play an important role in determining what you are worth in today's job market.

11. **Individuals who periodically "see the boss" about their salary will be more highly valued by their employers as well as receive higher salaries.** Most employers report how well a job candidate negotiates his or her salary largely sets the tone for how well they will do on the job. A similar principle operates in the case of asking for a raise. How well you present your case for a raise and the degree to which you are willing to work with the employer in reaching agreement should enhance your value in the eyes of your employer. After all, meeting with the boss about a raise is, in effect, a meeting to discuss how your past accomplishments and projected future performance should best be rewarded in terms of additional salary and benefits. Approached properly, this meeting stresses how valuable

you are to the employer. You become remembered as one of the most important players on the team, someone who should be retained at considerable cost. Conversely, those who do not periodically "see the boss" about a raise will probably receive minimum raises. You literally have to talk well about money in order to get more money from your boss.

12. **Expect limits on how large a raise you will receive, regardless of how well you handle the question of salary.** Most employers work under budgetary constraints when it comes to compensation questions. In small organizations, opportunities for career advancement tend to be limited and salaries tend to be less than in large organizations. Since salaries may quickly plateau within a few years in such organizations, you may have little room to negotiate a new salary. In such cases you may want to focus on developing a creative pay incentive scheme, acquiring stock options, or requiring employer contributions to a 401(k) Plan. In larger organizations, which have a more expanded promotion hierarchy, you may want to tie the issue of a salary raise to a promotion.

13. **"Seeing the boss" about compensation will occur more frequently in the future.** The old once-a-year performance or salary review will increasingly give way to employee-initiated compensation review sessions with their bosses. This may occur two or three times during the year, depending on how frequently one's job changes or what new contributions the employee makes to the organization.

Taken together, the compensation myths, realities, and trends argue for a particular approach to getting a raise in seven days. In subsequent chapters we outline how you can incorporate these realities and trends into your own approach to getting the raise you want in as short a time possible.

3

Test Your Salary I.Q. And Compensation Value

Just how well prepared are you to ask for a raise or get a promotion? Do you know how to prepare for a salary meeting? What will you take to the meeting? What do you plan to say? How do you plan to follow-up? Are you a salary savvy employee or do you commit common salary sins?

Take the Salary Savvy Test

Complete the following exercise by circling the number to the right that best represents your response according to this scale:

5 = strongly agree (Yes)
4 = agree
3 = maybe
2 = disagree
1 = strongly disagree (No)

	Yes				No
1. I know I'm fairly compensated for the work I do.	5	4	3	2	1
2. I usually have no problem talking about salaries, benefits, raises, and promotions with my bosses.	5	4	3	2	1
3. When meeting with my boss to discuss compensation, I bring to the meeting a list of "must ask" questions that deal with salary, benefits, raises, and promotions—and I ask them.	5	4	3	2	1
4. I know what I'm really worth in today's job market and can explain my worth to my boss.	5	4	3	2	1
5. I can quickly find out what people in other organizations are making for the same type of work I'm doing.	5	4	3	2	1
6. I know how salaries are figured in my company.	5	4	3	2	1
7. I have a good idea what others make in my company.	5	4	3	2	1
8. I know what percentage of my total compensation consists of benefits versus gross salary.	5	4	3	2	1
9. I understand how 401(k) plans, profit sharing, and pensions operate.	5	4	3	2	1

10. I know how much my benefits translate into before- and after-tax dollars.   5   4   3   2   1

11. I'm prepared to discuss at length with my boss various benefit options that will be advantageous to both me and the company.   5   4   3   2   1

12. I work in an organization that has a regular salary review process which is tied to a semi-annual or annual performance appraisal.   5   4   3   2   1

13. I regularly review and re-value my job to see if the scope of my work has expanded beyond the original position description for which I was hired.   5   4   3   2   1

TOTAL SCORE   [   ]

If your total score is 40 points or fewer, you're a good candidate for being under-compensated; you need to work on developing your "salary savvy" skills. If you score a perfect 75, congratulations; you are probably doing very well in the compensation department and may not need the advice found in this book. You're probably already a salary savvy employee!

What Is Your Compensation Worth?

Before you approach your employer about a raise or promotion, you should take an inventory of what you already negotiated when you accepted the position as well as agreements you reached in previous discussions about raises and promotions with your boss. This inventory should result in giving you a comprehensive picture of your current compensation situation. It also should result in giving you a total dollar value of your complete compensation package.

Knowing what you're worth in today's job market involves calculating a total compensation package—salary, benefits, and perks. According to the U.S. Department of Labor, the average worker receives nearly 45 percent of total compensation in forms other than base salary. While most of this extra compensation is in the form of mandatory social security contributions, many other benefits and perks can add up to a consider-able amount of compensation. At the same time, much of this extra com-pensation may be tax-free which further increases its overall dollar value. For example, the total value of employer-provided life insurance should be calculated in terms of what it would cost you if you had to pur-

> **Be sure you inventory your total compensation package (calculate its dollar value) before you approach your boss for a raise or promotion.**

chase the life insurance with your after tax dollars (i.e, a $400 premium may actually cost you $520 with after tax dollars and thus should be valued accordingly). Before you negotiate a salary or see your boss about a raise or promotion, be sure to take into consideration all elements that comprise your compensation package. Keep in mind that most elements may be negotiable. Some elements, such as supplemental pay options, may be more negotiable than base salary which for some employers may be relatively rigid in structure.

Use the following checklist to inventory your total compensa-tion package. Start by asking yourself these five questions:

1. Which compensation elements are most important to me?

2. Which elements does the employer offer?

3. How does each element with this company translate into real (after tax) dollars for me?

4. Which elements are negotiable with my employer?

5. How open is my employer to incorporating new elements in my compensation package or developing incentive pay schemes.

COMPENSATION ELEMENT	Dollar Equivalent	Very Important		Not Important		

Direct/Cash Compensation

❑ Base salary	$ _____	5	4	3	2	1
❑ Bonuses	$ _____	5	4	3	2	1
❑ Cash in lieu of certain benefits	$ _____	5	4	3	2	1
❑ Commissions	$ _____	5	4	3	2	1
❑ Overtime	$ _____	5	4	3	2	1
❑ Signing bonus	$ _____	5	4	3	2	1

Benefits

❑ Cafeteria plan	$ _____	5	4	3	2	1

- ❏ Reimbursement
  accounts $ _____   5   4   3   2   1
- ❏ Insurance
  - ❏ Medical $ _____   5   4   3   2   1
  - ❏ Dental $ _____   5   4   3   2   1
  - ❏ Life $ _____   5   4   3   2   1
  - ❏ Disability $ _____   5   4   3   2   1
- ❏ Financial/Retire-
  ment Plan:
  - ❏ 401(k) plan $ _____   5   4   3   2   1
  - ❏ Simplified
    Employee
    Pension (SEP) $ _____   5   4   3   2   1
  - ❏ Cash or deferred
    arrangement
    (CODA) $ _____   5   4   3   2   1
  - ❏ Pension or
    annuity $ _____   5   4   3   2   1
  - ❏ Profit sharing $ _____   5   4   3   2   1
  - ❏ Stock options $ _____   5   4   3   2   1
- ❏ Days off:
  - ❏ Vacation days $ _____   5   4   3   2   1
  - ❏ Sick leave days $ _____   5   4   3   2   1
  - ❏ Personal leave
    days $ _____   5   4   3   2   1
- ❏ Child care:
  - ❏ On-site $ _____   5   4   3   2   1

❑ Backup $_____   5   4   3   2   1

Perks

❑   Flex-time $_____   5   4   3   2   1

❑   Tuition
    reimbursement $_____   5   4   3   2   1

❑   Free parking $_____   5   4   3   2   1

❑   Car allowance $_____   5   4   3   2   1

❑   Cell phone $_____   5   4   3   2   1

❑   Free meals $_____   5   4   3   2   1

❑   Travel
    reimbursement $_____   5   4   3   2   1

❑   Company credit
    card $_____   5   4   3   2   1

❑   Frequent flier miles $_____   5   4   3   2   1

❑   Laptop computer $_____   5   4   3   2   1

❑   Upgraded
    business travel $_____   5   4   3   2   1

❑   Free or discounted
    memberships or
    services (shopping,
    health, financial,
    travel, events) $_____   5   4   3   2   1

❑   Discounts on
    company products $_____   5   4   3   2   1

❑   Sabbaticals $_____   5   4   3   2   1

❑   Community
    involvement $_____   5   4   3   2   1

❑   Incentive trips $_____   5   4   3   2   1

❑   Moving expenses $_____   5   4   3   2   1

❑ Office with
    a window $ _____   5   4   3   2   1

SUBTOTAL | $ |

Before tax dollars
savings $ _____

TOTAL | $ |

Whether you are looking for a job, negotiating a salary with a new employer, and talking about a raise or promotion with your boss, be sure to do your homework on compensation. Don't be afraid to talk about money and money comparables with the employer. If you don't do your homework and speak up about compensation, you're likely to short-change yourself in both the short- and long-run.

What Would You Like to Be Making?

Once you know what your current compensation is worth, consider what you really would like to be making on your current job. Ask yourself these questions:

1. What is this position really worth?

2. Am I making the most I can in this position?

3. Have my actual duties and responsibilities changed to the point they justify promotion to a higher paying position?

4. Does my employer have other positions for which I am qualified?

5. Are my skills worth more elsewhere?

6. Are my personal financial needs and goals in line with my present and future projected earnings with this company or should I consider moving on to greener pastures?

7. Is my boss well aware of my accomplishments and rewards me accordingly?

8. Do I have the necessary skills to justify a salary raise?

9. What would I like to be making five years from now?

10. What's the likelihood my boss will give me what I want?

Your answers to these questions should help set the stage for developing a seven-day plan for salary success as outlined in subsequent chapters.

4

Your Seven Day Success Plan

Getting a raise is not all that difficult if you approach your employment situation in the right way. In subsequent chapters we outline a well focused plan that consists of ten specific steps you can take over a seven day period. If followed in sequence and in earnest, you should be able to turn what may be a routine but potentially disappointing situation into one that substantially increases your value in the eyes of your employer, as well as fattens your paycheck!

The Plan

Our seven day plan for salary success encompasses ten steps that represent a model for planning and implementing a well conceived salary raise strategy. It's a plan we believe all employees—and employers—can benefit from, one that represents "win-win" and "honest but not stupid" philosophies we have long adhered to—

clearly communicate your qualifications and contributions to employers and value them accordingly. It requires keeping focused on what's really important to both you and your boss—delivering performance. At the very least, it requires investing a few hours of time in doing research, developing strategies, and practicing effective communication scenarios. If you translate your time into money, then consider the time spent in developing and implementing your ten step salary plan to be a very wise investment—it could well result in generating thousands of dollars in additional income during the next few years.

> **Focus on what's really important to both you and your boss—delivering performance.**

The Steps

The ten steps to salary success include the following sets of activities focused on getting a raise in seven days:

1. **Analyze your situation:** Whatever you do, make sure you know what type of situation you face before you initiate salary discussions and negotiations. The old adage that "knowledge is power" is especially true when facing compensation issues—the more you know about your situation, potentially the more savvy you will be in handling the situation with your boss and company. Be sure you understand the company culture, your boss, salary and promotion practices, and larger inflation and compensation trends. For example, as we noted in Chapter 3, make sure you know the value of your current compensation package. If the company culture is one that tends to reward team efforts rather than individual

performance, be sure to develop a salary strategy that emphasizes your contribution to overall team performance rather than only on your "Lone Ranger" contributions. If your boss relies on his or her boss to make important decisions, make sure you approach your boss with useful information to be presented to his or her boss. If your boss tends to deal best with personnel issues on a Tuesday or Wednesday morning rather than on a Monday or Friday afternoon, schedule your meeting accordingly at his or her best times. If salary increases are tied to an annual performance appraisal, focus on the criteria outlined in the appraisal. If nationwide statistics point out that the annual rate of inflation is 1.5 percent and the average annual salary increment is 3.5 percent, as it was in 1998, know that you are facing a situation in which an employer may not want to increase your salary above either of these "average" figures. If you are qualified for another position that pays more and is open, consider the possibility of talking about a promotion to that position with your boss. These "situational factors" may play a central role in how effective you will be in dealing with the compensation issue.

2. **Know what you're really worth:** You may quickly discover that both you and your boss lack the same knowledge—what you are really worth in today's job market. As a result, your boss may give you a raise based upon what he or she "feels" you are worth—reflecting a combination of your current salary, what others are making in the organization, and the raise you received last year. This myopic view of compensation fails to take into consideration the going market rate for someone with your skills and experience—salary comparisons

with the competition. In the end, your worth should be a combination of the following calculations:

1. What others in comparable positions in comparable organizations are making with your level of skills and experience.

2. What you are making in comparison to others in your organization.

3. What you would like to make and without which you are willing to quit your job.

The more information you have on your real value, the better you will be able to talk with your boss about your future compensation package.

3. **Consider your options:** While most people would like to make more money in their current job, they often do not receive major salary increases regardless of how well they perform or present a strong case to their boss. In many organizations, salaries for certain positions may quickly plateau and thus annual salary increments at best reflect annual cost of living increases. If you encounter this situation, you may want to consider other options, such as seek a promotion to a higher paying position within the company, change the value of your benefits, or look for employment elsewhere. Leaving one employer for another employer can result in a substantial increase in compensation (think in terms of at least 15 percent—less than that may not be worth the trouble of moving from one employer to another unless the job is particularly attractive for non-monetary reasons). What-

ever the case, make sure you consider your options. What else, for example, can you do in the organization? Do you have an exit strategy prior to meeting with your boss, such as conducting a preliminary job search online by posting your resume on a site that ensures you anonymity?

4. **Develop a strategy for talking money to power:** Meetings and their outcomes don't just happen—unless you want to be at a disadvantage. Any meeting involving salary should be well planned and involve a well thought-out strategy and agenda (Step #6). Your plan of action is your salary **strategy**. What you want to say and in what sequence is your salary **agenda**. Hopefully, you've also developed a long-term strategy relating to salary—what it is you plan to achieve throughout the year in order to justify a higher salary. When these two strategies meet, you'll be in a good position to talk money to power.

> Develop a long-term strategy relating to salary—what it is you plan to achieve throughout the year in order to justify a higher salary.

5. **Schedule a timely meeting:** Timing is everything! If your boss does not schedule an annual or semi-annual salary review or performance appraisal tied to compensation, take the initiative to schedule your own salary review meeting. Schedule this meeting a few days prior to the actual meeting. Also, choose an appropriate time to meet—ideally not on a busy Monday or Friday. The best time to meet is just after one of your major accom-

plishments has been communicated to your boss—you
just landed a major account; you saved the company
thousands of dollars with a new financial or management
approach; you brought a project in under cost or you
completed it early; you pioneered a new product line that
proved very profitable; or you developed a program that
expanded the company's client base. Rather than catalog
this important accomplishment for some future meeting
where you must quantify your performance for the year,
consider seizing this important moment by asking for a
raise. You will get a lot more mileage out of your current
accomplishment now than if you wait for several more
months when this accomplishment may no longer seem
as important to the employer. Storing your accomplishments like a squirrel stores nuts is not the best way to get
a raise; store some, but feast on others. Approaching the
boss as an obvious, and hopefully invaluable, performer
sets the stage in your favor. Do basic research on salary
comparables before scheduling a meeting with your boss.
Between the time you schedule the meeting and when
you actually meet, prepare yourself well for the meeting.
Detail how you want the meeting to proceed (Step #6)
and identify what you plan to say and do (Steps #7-8).

6. **Structure the situation to your advantage:** He who
   sets the agenda will have a major influence on the
   outcomes of the meeting. Therefore, it is to your advantage to bring as much structure to this meeting as possible. One of the best techniques is to develop a one-page
   "talking paper" which, in effect, structures the agenda for
   the meeting. This paper focuses attention on the key
   issues you wish to address with your boss. Each point
   should be related to a set of questions which hopefully

elicit the right answers for you. The old adage that "half of the solution to a problem is found in how you frame the question" should work in your favor. Your talking paper should play a major role in structuring the discussion around the outcomes you hope to achieve. If nothing else, it impresses upon your employer that you are well prepared and serious about dealing with the salary question. You know your value and therefore you wish to be compensated accordingly. Many employers respect such thoughtful initiatives.

7. **Develop a 3-minute "Perfect Salary Pitch":** *"Why should I give you a raise? What will it cost me?"* These are the first two questions an employer will ask himself when confronted with the issue of compensation. If you can't succinctly answer the first question in three minutes, perhaps you shouldn't be talking about money. You must be prepared to provide your boss with a rationale to justify your salary request. One of the best ways to handle this question is to develop a 3-minute "Perfect Salary Pitch." This statement clearly communicates to your employer why you deserve a raise or promotion. It includes three basic elements: (1) your top five accomplishments during the past year; (2) what you are currently doing for the employer; and (3) what you plan to achieve in the coming year. Everything mentioned in your "Perfect Salary Pitch" must be employer-centered rather than self-centered—it tells the employer what you are doing for the company to justify your current and

> **You must be prepared to provide your boss with a rationale to justify your salary request.**

future salary. Do not try to memorize this pitch. If you do, you will most likely sound insincere. Your pitch should be an extemporaneous statement centered around key talking points that comprise your unique "Perfect Salary Pitch." It must clearly focus on your value in relationship to the organization's goals.

8. **Anticipate objections to your pitch:** Regardless of how convincing you may believe you are in justifying your salary request, you can expect objections to your salary pitch. Most objections will relate to the three standard reasons employers give for not increasing salaries:

   ▪ not in the budget

   ▪ exceeds what others make in comparable positions within the organization

   ▪ can't justify it to the next level of management

Since none of these objections relate to your performance or your specific contributions to the organization, they should be relatively easy to deal with from your well focused perspective. At this point it's important to keep on message—your exceptional talent in exchange for more compensation. As with your "Perfect Salary Pitch," be prepared to address each objection with an employer-centered rationale that reinforces the themes emphasized in your "Perfect Salary Pitch." Let your boss know that you have greater value than he or she has heretofore recognized. Remember, you are an economic commodity that may be purchased at a higher price should you decide to look elsewhere for employment opportunities. Employers know this is a possibility and that it can be costly to them should you decide to make such a move. The more your boss knows just how valuable you are to the organization, the more receptive he or she will be to your salary request. Respond to such objections by repeating the major themes in your perfect salary pitch. This is the time when redundancy becomes a virtue!

9. **Close and follow-up with impact:** Know when it's time to close the salary meeting. Such a meeting should take from 30 to 45 minutes. Since you have attempted to control the agenda with your talking paper, you should be able to move the discussion from point to point and finally to closure. Ideally, a good closing should result in a new salary figure that meets your expectations. If this happens, be sure to express your sincere gratitude to the employer and reiterate your commitment to performing well in the year ahead. Assure your boss that you enjoy working for him or her. Remember, how you handle yourself in this meeting may influence how well you get along with your boss in the future. If, for example, you become too pushy and thus appear greedy by only seeming to be concerned about making more money, you may quickly lose value in the eyes of your boss. You may be seen as someone who no longer "fits into" the organization. Your boss may conclude you will be more trouble than you are worth by continuing to push the salary issue. Therefore, you may be invited to look

> How you handle yourself in this meeting may influence how well you get along with your boss in the future.

elsewhere for employment—for a job that is a better "fit." If, on the other hand, you do not reach closure in this meeting, close the meeting by:

- Summarizing the major points of your discussion.

- Reiterating the major themes in your "Perfect Salary Pitch"—redundancy continues to be a virtue even at the end stage of this meeting.

- Reaching agreement on what should happen next, such as scheduling another meeting at which time you will finalize your salary.

Keep your options open by asking to meet soon to further discuss your salary concerns. Then follow-up with any additional information that will strengthen your case.

10. **Then do what you said you're worth.** You should always approach compensation with a long-term view. You must deliver what you say you will deliver and document it accordingly for your boss. If not, you may not be able to continue justifying your last raise nor push for another raise. Salary meetings can take place every three or six months, or once a year. At each meeting, you want to be in the strongest position possible. You want the content of your "Perfect Salary Pitch" to constantly change in the direction of what you last said you planned to accomplish in the future. Be able to start your next salary meeting with a key transitional phrase that updates your boss on what you've accomplished since your last

meeting and moves this process forward—*"I'm happy to report that since we last met, I've been able to . . ."* You talk about your new accomplishments and how you've added greater value to the organization since your last meeting. Again, you remain focused on what's really important to both you and your boss. You made promises in the last meeting; now you must document your performance. If you made promises you could not keep, you will lose your credibility in the eyes of your employer, regardless of how skillful you are in structuring a salary meeting and delivering a "Perfect Salary Pitch." At this point, your pitch and your performance must match!

The Performance

Organizing and implementing a 10-step plan to salary success requires keeping focused on what's really important to employers in today's highly competitive economy. In each step of your plan, you need to achieve a certain level of functional redundancy—repeating in different words and phrases a similar message about what you have done in the past, what you are doing at present, and what you plan to do in the future for the employer. The message must be employer-centered. Countering any objections that might be raised about your salary request, your message must communicate that the employer will gain additional value from you that will more than justify your salary increase. If you can keep focused on your message in this manner, you should have an excellent chance of getting a raise in seven days!

Part II

10 Steps to Salary Success

5

Analyze Your Situation

What exactly is your salary situation with your current employer? Do you know how compensation is handled within your organization? Are raises normally decided by management and then announced to employees by their bosses or do employees have some input into the compensation process through, for example, an annual performance appraisal or periodic salary review? How effective have you been in the past in influencing your boss to take actions that benefit you? Are you a recognized performer who regularly promotes your achievements? Can you take on new responsibilities? What factors within your organization will most likely determine your future compensation?

Knowledge Is Power

The problem with many employees is that they approach the salary question high on motivation (*"I really need a raise"*) but low on useful and usable information that appeals to their target audience —the boss (*"I deserve a raise because I have done the following for the company"*). They also fail to regularly communicate a significant track record of actions that persuades employers to reward performance with raises and promotions. As a result, many employees tend to communicate self-centered need and greed (*"I need to make more because I just purchased a new car with high monthly payments"* or *"We have a new baby due in July"*) or a beggar mentality (*"Please help me with my finances"*) which the employer may interpret as financial irresponsibility (*"You really shouldn't do things you can't afford—I don't feel responsible for your financial irresponsibility"*). Such a high motivation approach may actually diminish your value in the eyes of your employer.

Instead, you need to communicate useful information that motivates the employer to increase your salary.

> **Make a powerful statement about your performance in relationship to the company's goals.**

Knowledge is power when dealing with the salary issue. The more you know about yourself, your employer, the company, and the competition, the stronger your position in making your case for a raise or promotion. You need good, solid information that especially appeals to your employer. The safest assumption is that the most useful information you can give the employer will focus on the employer's bottomline—what you are contributing above and beyond what is normally expected from your current position. In other words, your information needs to be performance-oriented—communicate loud and clear that you are a valuable asset to the company. If they make you unhappy or lose you because of their salary shortsightedness, they may pay dearly in the long-run. That's your knowledge goal—make a powerful statement about your performance in relationship to the company's goals.

When Asking For a Raise May Get You More Than You Bargained For!

John was compelled to stop by his boss's office on Thursday to ask if he could meet with him on Monday to discuss something important that recently came up. His boss, Frank, said *"Sure . . . let's meet at 4:30pm on Monday."*

Frank was curious about this rather sudden request to get together with John. This wasn't like John who was usually very quiet and relatively compliant; taking initiative was not one of his strong points. Frank wondered what he was up to—getting married, discovered a procurement problem, or planning to quit his job? Maybe John is finally going to show some initiative by coming up with a solution to some of our serious purchasing problems!

On Monday at 4:30pm sharp John arrives at Frank's office. *"Are you free?"* he asks. *"Sure, come on in John. What's on your mind?"* Frank asks.

"Well, I have a bit of a problem. You know that car I've been driving for the past year? It was giving me some transmission problems. When I took it into the shop, they told me it would cost nearly $1000 to fix. So last week I started looking for another car. I came across this low mileage truck and decided to buy it. It's really nice. I didn't get much for my trade-in, and I had to take out a loan for the new truck. My monthly payments are now twice what they were before. My financial situation is kind of difficult, especially since I decided last Wednesday to move to a new apartment complex where the monthly payments are nearly $200 higher. I really need a raise. How much more can I expect to make this year?"

Frank looks John in the eye and says, *"I'm really sorry to hear you're getting in over your head financially. I don't mean to be your financial advisor, but had you asked me before you bought the truck or rented the new apartment, I would have given you the same advice I got when I was your age—you need to live within your means, manage your money better, or find a job that pays a lot more than what you're getting here. The type of raise you need to finance your new lifestyle is not in the cards this year, and probably not even next year."*

John looks somewhat dejected but he's not ready to give up yet. *"Yeah, I knew I was getting in over my head, but I was hoping I would get a nice salary increase to make up the difference. Are there some other things I can do here to make more money? What about overtime? What about another position that pays more?"*

Frank tries to empathize with John, but he gets increasingly irritated with this self-destructive line of conversation. *"John, those alternatives are not in the cards either. I'm glad you brought this up now rather than wait another two months for your annual performance appraisal. Let's be honest with each other. You're already having trouble keeping up with your current work. In fact, you've been getting behind with everything, and our whole purchasing system seems to be in disarray. I'm sure some of these problems are due to your personal circumstances. But I'm not the one you need to come to for financial help. I don't give loans to employees, and I'm not about to give you a raise just because you need more money to support your new lifestyle. Unless I see some real improvement in your work soon, you may have to start looking for another job which may or may not pay more than this one. So let's get on with doing a better job so we can eventually talk about a raise based upon your improved performance."*

Taken aback at this surprising and rather ominous response, John replies, *"You're right. I can't expect you to solve my financial problems. I need to do something before I really get in over my head."* He thanks Frank for his time.

Four weeks later John turns in his resignation and finds a new job that pays less but gives him more flexibility to moonlight as a security guard. He's still struggling to make ends meet. He doesn't know what he really wants to do other than find a job that will more than pay the bills, especially since his lifestyle has changed again—he just got married and will soon become a father.

On Your Own

Assuming you are not part of a collective bargaining process, such as a union that annually negotiates compensation packages for its members, you're largely on your own in affecting your company's compensation system. At the very least, you need to take certain actions that result in renegotiating your current compensation package in the form of a raise and/or promotion.

What exactly do you need to do in order to get started in the right direction? Let's begin by taking an inventory of key information you need at this stage. These are items you need to consider when getting prepared to deal with the compensation issue.

Develop a Thirteen-Point Information Checklist

Before you invest time and effort in asking for a raise or promotion, begin gathering information on these thirteen important elements that may affect your compensation future:

❑ Company handbook on personnel procedures. (It may outline the company's system of benefits and procedures on dealing with raises and promotions)

❑ Your employment contract or letter that spells out the terms of your employment. (Does it include exit provisions, such as a severance package, should you decide to resign?)

❑ Documentation on your company benefits, such as health, life, and disability insurance; profit sharing and 401(k) plans; pension program; and backup child care. What are they really worth and how much are you versus the employer contributing?

❑ Non-reimbursed costs of being an employee that may be reimbursed by other employers (uniforms, travel, meals, overtime, books, education and training, laptop computer, software, telephone).

❑ Value of current compensation package (see your calculations on pages 42-44 of Chapter 3).

❑ Special recognitions or awards you've received from your boss and/or clients during the year.

❑ Effectiveness of self-promotion throughout the year—how well you have communicated your performance and value to your boss on a regular basis.

❑ Assessment of your boss's approach to compensation issues—open minded, raises objections, avoids discussion, deals best with issues early in the morning, or other behavioral characteristics you need to consider before approaching him or her about a raise or promotion.

❑ The company's current economic health. What's its profit/loss situation at present? If profitable, to what degree does the company share its most recent wealth with its employees? Profit sharing? Bonuses? Raises?

❑ Assessment of your contribution to the company's profits in terms of the actual dollars your performance contributed to the bottomline.

❑ The degree—on a scale of 1 to 10—to which you are liked, respected, and valued within the company.

❑ Annual average level of inflation (percentage) on a local, regional, and/or national level.

❑ Annual average wage increases (percentage) at a local, regional, and/or national level.

Take the items on this checklist seriously as well as incorporate additional ones that appear important to your organization. After all, much of this information may eventually be incorporated into your "talking paper" as outlined in Chapter 10 on structuring the situation as well as included in your powerful "Perfect Salary Pitch" in Chapter 11. The items in this thirteen-point checklist are the building blocks used by savvy salary negotiators in putting together a well-reasoned and documented case for why they should receive the raise or promotion they request from their boss. These items make a powerful case for giving you the raise you feel you both earned and deserve.

Evaluate Your Current Level of Job Satisfaction

We also recommend that you evaluate your current level of job satisfaction and the structure of your work environment. Are you a happy camper? Has your job progressed in the manner you expected? Are there certain things you would like to change about your job? Have you taken on additional responsibilities that are not reflected in your compensation? Would your employer be willing to give you some intangible benefits that would make the job a better "fit" for you? There are things you like or dislike about your current job; some may involve job restructuring while others are more window dressing in nature. While they may not be easily measured in terms dollars and cents, nonetheless, they are important to your overall job satisfaction and performance. You may be able to include many of them when you "see the boss" about a raise or promotion.

	Very Important				Not Important
1. Job or position title	1	2	3	4	5
2. Work environment	1	2	3	4	5
3. Management style	1	2	3	4	5
4. Entrepreneurism/initiative	1	2	3	4	5
5. Flexible work hours	1	2	3	4	5
6. Telecommuting option	1	2	3	4	5
7. Professional growth	1	2	3	4	5
8. Challenging work	1	2	3	4	5
9. Opportunity to have own projects	1	2	3	4	5
10. Opportunity to travel	1	2	3	4	5

For example, you may want to negotiate a new job title because it will enhance your overall professional image. It costs the employer nothing to change your title from "Secretary" to "Administrative Assistant" or from "Publicist" to "Director of Communications," but it could mean a few thousand dollars in additional salary when you seek a position with another employer who views your new and improved title as one of great responsibility and experience. The same is true for "entrepreneurism." If the current management style is more top-down command and control than participatory and entrepreneurial, and you best thrive as a self-starter in entrepreneurial settings, it costs the employer nothing—but potentially could benefit the organization tremendously—by aligning you with a different management style that is more compatible with your work style.

You may want to convert several of these items into a series of job preference statements:

Job Preferences

1. I prefer the following job title: _____

2. I would like my work environment to encompass the following elements: _____
    _____

3. I would like to eliminate the following from my job and work environment: _____
    _____

4. My work would best thrive in the following management environment: _____
    _____

5. I would like to have greater responsibility for doing the following: _____

    _____

6. I prefer working with people who have the following characteristics: _____

    _____

7. If I could change my working hours, they would be the following: _____

8. I could be more productive if my office looked like or included the following: _____

    _____

9. The three most important things that would really keep me happy and productive at this company during the next five years include:

    A. _____
    B. _____
    C. _____

10. If I could choose the three perfect projects to work on over the next year, they would be:

    A. _____
    B. _____
    C. _____

You may want to incorporate several of these preference statements in your one-page "Talking Paper" (Chapter 10) and in your "Perfect Salary Pitch" (Chapter 11). Like the thirteen-point information checklist outlined at the beginning of this chapter, these preference statements are important building blocks for savvy salary negotiators.

Current Compensation Package

One of the most important parts of knowing your situation is to calculate the total value of your current compensation package. You began this process in Chapter 3 (pages 42-44) when you inventoried your total compensation package and translated each element into a dollar equivalent. Now, take this exercise one step further by projecting what you would like to see happen after you "see the boss" about your raise and/or promotion:

	Current	Desired	LEVEL OF PROBABILITY				
			Negotiable			Non-negotiable	

Direct/Cash Compensation

❑ Base salary	$ _____	$ _____	5	4	3	2	1
❑ Bonus	$ _____	$ _____	5	4	3	2	1
❑ Cash in lieu of certain benefits	$ _____	$ _____	5	4	3	2	1
❑ Commissions	$ _____	$ _____	5	4	3	2	1
❑ Overtime	$ _____	$ _____	5	4	3	2	1

Benefits

❑ Cafeteria plan	$ _____	$ _____	5	4	3	2	1
❑ Reimbursement accounts	$ _____	$ _____	5	4	3	2	1
❑ Insurance							
❑ Medical	$ _____	$ _____	5	4	3	2	1

❑ Dental $ _____ $ _____   5   4   3   2   1

❑ Life $ _____ $ _____   5   4   3   2   1

❑ Disability $ _____ $ _____   5   4   3   2   1

❑ Financial/Retire-
   ment Plan:

   ❑ 401(k) plan $ _____ $ _____   5   4   3   2   1

   ❑ Simplified
      Employee
      Pension (SEP) $ _____ $ _____ 5   4   3   2   1

   ❑ Cash or deferred
      arrangement
      (CODA) $ _____ $ _____   5   4   3   2   1

   ❑ Pension or
      annuity $ _____ $ _____   5   4   3   2   1

   ❑ Profit sharing $ _____ $ _____ 5   4   3   2   1

   ❑ Stock options $ _____ $ _____ 5   4   3   2   1

❑ Days off:

   ❑ Vacation days $ _____ $ _____ 5   4   3   2   1

   ❑ Sick leave days $ _____ $ _____ 5   4   3   2   1

   ❑ Personal leave
      days $ _____ $ _____   5   4   3   2   1

❑ Child care:

   ❑ On-site $ _____ $ _____   5   4   3   2   1

   ❑ Backup $ _____ $ _____   5   4   3   2   1

Perks

❑	Flex-time	$ _____	$ _____	5	4	3	2	1
❑	Tuition reimbursement	$ _____	$ _____	5	4	3	2	1
❑	Free parking	$ _____	$ _____	5	4	3	2	1
❑	Car allowance	$ _____	$ _____	5	4	3	2	1
❑	Cell phone	$ _____	$ _____	5	4	3	2	1
❑	Free meals	$ _____	$ _____	5	4	3	2	1
❑	Travel reimbursement	$ _____	$ _____	5	4	3	2	1
❑	Company credit card	$ _____	$ _____	5	4	3	2	1
❑	Airline miles	$ _____	$ _____	5	4	3	2	1
❑	Laptop computer	$ _____	$ _____	5	4	3	2	1
❑	Upgraded business travel	$ _____	$ _____	5	4	3	2	1
❑	Free or discounted memberships or services (shopping, health, financial, travel, events)	$ _____	$ _____	5	4	3	2	1
❑	Discounts on company products	$ _____	$ _____	5	4	3	2	1
❑	Sabbaticals	$ _____	$ _____	5	4	3	2	1
❑	Incentive trips	$ _____	$ _____	5	4	3	2	1
❑	Moving expenses	$ _____	$ _____	5	4	3	2	1
❑	Office with a window	$ _____	$ _____	5	4	3	2	1

❑ Other:

_____	$ _____	$ _____	5	4	3	2	1
_____	$ _____	$ _____	5	4	3	2	1
_____	$ _____	$ _____	5	4	3	2	1
_____	$ _____	$ _____	5	4	3	2	1
_____	$ _____	$ _____	5	4	3	2	1

SUBTOTALS $ _____ $ _____

Before tax dollars
savings $ _____ $ _____

TOTALS $ _____ $ _____

Company Culture and Salary Procedures

Every company has its own culture which defines the way things get done. This culture suggests certain "do's" and "taboos" about raises and promotions. Consider, for example, what are supposed to be tightly held company secrets between the company and each individual employee. Such secrets are not to be shared amongst employees. In most organizations it's considered taboo to talk about your salary and/or raise with fellow employees; indeed, doing so may get you fired! Salaries and raises are supposed to be very private and secret affairs—only to be discussed between the employee and the employer and perhaps shared within the employee's immediate family. Performance appraisals also are usually kept secret—only between the employer and the individual employee. In many organizations the culture tends to be very formal, procedural, and competitive whereas in other organizations the culture is very informal, congenial, supportive, and cooperative. Make sure you understand your organizational culture and how it affects raises and promotions. If you don't, you may be in for some surprises that could have a negative impact on your future with the company. Ask yourself these questions:

- What is the proper way to pose the question of a raise or promotion?

- Is this something I initiate with my immediate supervisor or should I check with personnel on procedures?

- Is it okay to discuss salaries, raises, and promotions with my colleagues?

- Does the organization publicize salary information, make it available upon request, or keep it secret?

- When does the company usually consider raises and promotions?

- Does each employee have an anniversary date at which time raises are discussed or are raises only considered as part of an annual performance appraisal or salary review?

- Does the company prefer giving annual bonuses over percentage raises or vice versa?

- How much input does the company expect from its employees when it's time to figure raises?

- Who really has the power to make final decisions regarding raises and promotions?

The Boss

Chances are your boss or immediate supervisor will play a key role in determining your raise or promotion. However, the extent of his or her role may vary depending on the organization. In many cases, your boss or immediate supervisor will be empowered to initiate the process, but all final decisions regarding raises and promotions will be made elsewhere—by another level of management or by a board. Consequently, don't assume you are talking to the person who has the power to make final decisions. Any salary requests may require that your boss present a proposal to someone else and the final decision may take some time— perhaps a week or two. If this is the case, you should approach your boss with the knowledge that he or she will need a good rationale to present your case to others. Your job is to make your boss look good in the eyes of his or her boss when your case is presented for a final decision. At the very least, you want your boss to become your advocate to his/her boss.

> **Your job is to make your boss look good in the eyes of his or her boss when your case is presented for a final decision.**

So how well do you really know your boss? Ask yourself these questions in preparation for the critical salary raise or promotion meeting with your boss:

1. How good is my relationship with my boss? Does he/she respect and trust me as well as have confidence in my judgment?

2. How easily can I approach my boss about a raise? Do we talk frankly and honestly or must we watch what

we say and try to manipulate each other?

3. Knowing my boss's habits, when is the best time to schedule a meeting to discuss a raise or promotion?

4. Knowing my boss's habits, are there certain times and situations I should try to avoid when scheduling this meeting?

5. Does my boss usually listen to me and take my ideas seriously?

6. Has my boss given me regular feedback on my performance and made suggestions on how I can improve my work?

7. What objections might my boss have to my request for a raise and/or promotion?

8. To whom does my boss report?

9. How difficult might it be for my boss to present my case to his/her boss?

10. What can I say or do that will best help my boss present my case to his/her boss?

Whatever you do, make sure you understand your boss, especially how he or she fits into the whole salary equation and relates to you. Without a solid understanding of these relationships, you may have difficulty getting beyond the initial salary discussion stage.

Effectiveness of Your Self-Promotion

One of the best ways to position yourself for a raise is to engage in self-promotion on a regular basis. A form of personal public relations (PR), this involves communicating to your boss and other powerful people who can make a difference in your compensation what it is you are doing that contributes greater value to the organization. It means keeping in touch with your boss about you and your work. It also involves be-coming likable by personalizing your relationship with your boss—talk about your family, your hobbies, and your special interests and occasion-ally go out together for lunch or spe-cial events. Remember, it's harder to say "no" to someone you like than to someone you hardly know. At the same time, you want to become more

> **One of the best ways to position yourself for a raise is to engage in self-promotion on a regular basis.**

and more professional by letting your boss know what's happening in your department or on your special projects. Don't just catalog this information and reveal it all at once during a formal perfor-mance appraisal or salary review. Without becoming are PR nuisance, mention lots of little things throughout the year. For example:

- You just made a contact that you hope will result in new business for the company.

- You discovered a new way to publicize the company's services which should save it several thousands of dollars in advertising costs.

- You designed a unique database that will pinpoint customer interests and generate automatic follow-up mechanisms for doing up-sales on a new product line.

- You just talked with one of the company's most valued clients about developing a new $300,000 project.

These are little things that happen on a daily basis but the cumulative affect is to communicate to your boss that you are getting things done. Avoid being overbearing or wasting a lot of your boss's time by engaging in obvious self-promotion activities. Your boss, too, is probably a busy person. If you pester him or her with your personal PR, these activities can backfire and they may be held against you. You want to regularly communicate to your boss that you are a performer who is active, enthusiastic, and focused on getting results. Most important of all, you are a valuable asset the company would not want to lose over an issue of compensation. Therefore, you need to be regularly rewarded for your dedication and performance.

Be sure to assess how well you are doing in the PR department. Have you been actively promoting yourself and your performance throughout the year? If you are well liked by your boss both personally and professionally, you'll be in a very good position to "see the boss" about a raise and/or promotion. Remember, it's hard to say "no" to someone you really like.

Job Growth and Taking On New Responsibilities

One of the best ways to get a salary raise is to volunteer to take on new responsibilities that will add greater value to the organization. However, before you do this, examine your current position in relation to its original job description. You need to assess to what degree your job has already grown beyond its original intent. You need to know whether or not you have taken on responsibilities that are not part of your job and for which you have not been adequately compensated. Ask yourself these questions:

1. What specific duties and responsibilities are assigned to this position?

2. How has my job expanded over the past year?

3. What additional responsibilities have I acquired that are normally not part of this position?

4. How do these additional responsibilities compare to comparable positions in other organizations?

5. How much are my additional responsibilities worth to my employer?

Once you've addressed these questions, you should consider what additional responsibilities you would like to add to your position and for which you would like to receive additional compensation. These are jobs you would like to take on for the purpose of expanding the value of your current position. However, before you do this, make sure you are currently doing your job according to expectations. If you volunteer to expand the scope of your work when you can't complete your current level of work, you will be viewed as someone who is irresponsible. Indeed, your boss may flatly tell you *"I really want you to do your current job better rather than take on new responsibilities. Let's get you up to speed before we even consider expanding your job!"* A case in point is the salary negotiation scenario involving John and Frank on pages 63-64.

Promotion Potential

Another major way of getting a raise is to be promoted to a higher paying position. Always keep this option in mind when you talk about a raise. If you work in a large organization that has various hierarchies of positions to which people get promoted, keep your eye on these other positions. It may be time to be considered for a promotion once one of these positions becomes vacant. At the same time, you may want to think about proposing the creation of a new position for which you are qualified. Take, for example, someone who has desktop publishing and graphics skills but is in a secretarial or administrative assistant position. This person would be wise to propose the creation of a new position, such as "desktop publisher and graphic artist" which could result in a significant increase in pay. This new position would involve a higher skill level and would contribute more to the company's bottomline.

> **Another major way of getting a raise is to be promoted to a higher paying position.**

Ask yourself these questions when considering a promotion option:

1. Am I performing at the top of my position?

2. Has my job already expanded to the point where it really should be considered a different position?

3. Do I have the experience and skills to qualify for another position in this organization?

4. Can I put together a good case for creating a new position

for which I am qualified and which will add value to the organization?

When gathering information about your situation, do so with a view toward creating a new position or occupying another higher paying position. This may be your time to go for a promotion that will move you into a new level of compensation.

The Company's Financial Health

If you work for a company that is relatively open about its finances, you should have a very good idea about its current profit and loss situation. However, if this information is not normally shared with employees, you may need to do some sleuthing to find out how well it's doing. Try doing some combination of the following:

1. Ask your boss about the health of the company: *"How has the company been doing this year?"*

2. Check with a few of your trusted co-workers: *"How do you think the company has been doing this year?"*

3. If it's a public company, research its stock prices and quarterly and annual reports.

4. Talk to a stock broker or the competition about how well the company is doing.

If your company is experiencing financial difficulties, chances are you will be in a weak position to ask for a raise. One of the legitimate employer objections will be that the company's current financial situation cannot justify such a raise. In this case, you may need to lower your immediate financial expectations and focus instead on promises of future rewards, such as stock options or bonuses. You also may want to explore opportunities with other employers, just in case your current employer starts downsizing and fails to turn around the business. You may find yourself in a very difficult employment situation as the declining company continues to experience losses, morale declines, and work shifts into a crisis management mode.

Let's hope your timing is right in relation to the company's financial health. If the company is doing well, ask yourself these questions:

1. What has been this company's pattern of "sharing the wealth" with its employees? Does it primarily reward its top executives and stockholders, or does it also share its profits with its employees through some combination of profit sharing, bonuses, and raises?

2. What portion of the increased profitability can be attributed to my efforts? For example, did I generate $200,000 in additional business this year and can I document this contribution for my boss?

Your Effectiveness

Be sure to compile evidence of your accomplishments. If you have an on-going PR strategy in which you regularly communicate to your boss "what's going on," you should have a substantial file of evidence to incorporate in your one-page talking paper (Chapter 10) and your "Perfect Salary Pitch" (Chapter 11). However, be careful how you present this information. Workload statistics and stories about your efforts are no substitute for specifying effectiveness, achievements, or outcomes for the organization. For example, rather than focus on the 200 new calls you made last month (your workload), outline how many calls resulted in new business that can be quantified as specific dollar outcomes (last month I opened seven new accounts that initially placed $30,000 in orders).

The Future

You also should assess your future with your current employer as well as the future of the company? Ask yourself these questions:

1. Where do you stand in relationship to others in the organization?

2. Are you advancing as rapidly as others who were hired after you?

3. Is your current job a good "fit" for your particular mix of interests, skills, and abilities?

4. Are there other things you would rather be doing than what you are currently doing in your job?

At the same time, consider the future of your employer:

1. Where does this company seem to be going over the next five years?

2. How will the company share its wealth with its employees?

3. Is this a growing company that will provide increased opportunities for its current employees?

4. Is this the type of place where I will enjoy growing my career?

External Trends

Understanding your situation also involves knowing where your salary stands in relationship to the average inflation rate and average salary increases. In 1998, for example, the average rate of inflation was 1.5 percent; the average increase in salary was 3.5 percent. Salaries out-paced the rate of inflation by 3 to 1 which meant salaries were generally on the rise after several years of falling behind the rate of inflation. Based on this data, in 1998 you would want to receive at least a 3.5 percent salary increase to be considered "average." Anything less than 3.5 percent should be interpreted as a below normal salary increase. Be sure you have this information before you "see your boss." Many employers do not want to be below average when it comes to compensating their employees; they want to be known as "competitive." And it is the competition that will ultimately give you greater value in the eyes of your employer.

6

Know What You're Really Worth

After you analyze your situation, you next need to calculate what you're really worth in today's job market. If you're like most employees, the last time you knew your market value was when you were hired. You were most likely hired near the going market rate because both you and the employer were familiar with salary comparables. But after a year or two on the job, you've probably lost touch with the salary market and thus may have fallen behind in compensation. You can and should correct this situation when you ask for a raise.

Falling Behind, Catching Up

After several months on the job, most employees no longer pay attention to their market value simply because they are no longer in the job market. Instead, they concentrate on doing their job and being rewarded with annual raises and bonuses which may or may not reflect their real market value. Many turn inward, comparing their current compensation to their previous earnings as well as speculating how their compensation and career advancement compare to that of others in the organization. Only when they go job hunting again do they become educated on their true market value. In the meantime, as new employees come on board with comparable skills and experience, they may be hired at a higher salary than you, because they and the employer know the current market value for recruiting new talent. The value of existing talent tends to follow its own internal logic—tends to be what current employees are willing to accept in the form of a raise plus their current salary.

The Job Market Reveals Going Rates and Ranges

While it may be interesting to learn what others in your organization are making, such information is not particularly useful for the purposes of getting a raise. You can assume your company, like many others, is filled with all kinds of salary inequities due to the way salaries have been determined in the past—negotiated individually and at different times and at different market rates. Knowing about such inequities will not help you improve your compensation situation—it will only upset you when you discover some people who seem to contribute less than you actually make more than you! Get over such inevitable inequities and, instead, concentrate on the most powerful information you can bring to the negotiation table—comparative market rates.

> Knowing what others in your organization make is not particularly useful for getting a raise. Salary inequities exist due to the way salaries have been determined in the past.

The current distribution of salaries within your organization probably reflects a combination of market forces and individual negotiation skills. The market value for C++ and Java programmers in 1998, for example, was $80,000; the market value for the same programmers hired in 1996 was closer to $40,000. Chances are C++ and Java programmers working in the same organization but hired at different times may be receiving very different salaries. And chances are that many of those programmers who were hired earlier but now know their real market value have been busy negotiating raises that bring them up to their current market value. But if they didn't check their real value by investigating what new recruits are currently being offered, chances are their compensation would lag significantly behind that of new recruits.

> The best way to determine what you're really worth is to research the current job market.

The best way to determine what you're really worth is to research the current job market. The job market will give you both salary rates and salary ranges. The good news is that you don't have to become a job candidate in order to get this information. As you will quickly discover, there are many sources of salary information that you can easily access to learn about your true market worth. Many of them are just a phone call away or a click or two on the Internet.

Check Key Studies and Printed Resources

Numerous studies are published each year on salaries and salary ranges. They are conducted by federal, state, and local government agencies; professional associations; employment firms; reporters; and academic researchers. They come in many different forms, from free quarterly government reports to expensive directories and specialized private studies on salaries and wages. Many of these studies are excellent resources for identifying general salary ranges whereas others are more specific and detailed for different positions within certain occupations. With a little time, patience, and money, you should be able to quickly access this data.

Keep in mind that most of these studies will be more or less useful. Some may seem too general in scope to apply to your specific situation; others may be specific but they fail to cover your geographic area. Overall, few of these studies may be comprehensive and detailed enough to relate to your specific situation. Nonetheless, they will give you some idea of the market ranges for salaries related to your particular occupational field.

We recommend eight sources and activities for acquiring useful information. Most encompass salary studies and reports:

1. **Visit your local library, especially the information or reference section.** Libraries and librarians tend to have a wealth of information on salaries in the form of directories and federal, state, and local government wage surveys. While you should search the library database for such information, be sure to ask a librarian for assistance. Many librarians are well aware of a variety of resources relating to salaries and wages and especially local studies that may be more relevant to your situation. Some of the most important directories revealing salary information include:

   ➤ *Amercan Salaries and Wages Survey:* Published annually by Gale Research (Helen S. Fisher, editor), this is the most comprehensive source on salary and wage data. It includes over 32,000 salaries for more than 4,500 occupational classifications in thousands of communities through the country. The directory's database includes nearly 300 government, business, and news sources. A rich resource for identifying salary ranges and locating salary surveys.

➤ *American Almanac of Jobs and Salaries:* Authored by John Wright and published by Avon Books, new editions of this popular book are published every two, three, or four years. Each edition includes salary information on numerous occupations. The salary data comes from numerous salary studies conducted by government agencies, professional associations, and private employment firms.

➤ *Occupational Outlook Handbook:* Look for the latest edition of the Department of Labor's biannual reference work, the *Occupational Outlook Handbook.* Each edition surveys nearly 250 major occupations that cover nearly 85 percent of all jobs in the United States. Individual occupational entries include information on salary ranges. While broad in scope, the salary information will give you a good idea of the upper and lower salary limits of your particular occupation.

➤ **Government studies:** Most major libraries catalog copies of various federal, state, and local government wage and salary surveys. Check with your librarian to see what's available, especially some of the publications and studies we identify on page 91.

2. **Contact a professional association relevant to your occupational field.** Most professional associations

conduct annual salary surveys of their members and
usually make this information available free to its
members or for a fee to nonmembers. This information
is often used by employers for recruitment purposes or
by members who are looking for jobs or calculating
raises. Employers hiring recent college graduates for
entry-level positions, for example, rely a great deal on
the annual salary survey conducted by the National
Association of Colleges and Em-
ployers (NACE). Indeed, this
survey has become the "bible"
for college recruiters who must
offer market sensitive salaries in
this highly competitive job market. While you can purchase this

**Most professional associa-
tions conduct annual salary
surveys of their members.**

study for nearly $200.00, you may be able to get access
to it through a college career center. The National
Association of Broadcasters also publishes an annual
compensation and fringe benefit report that outlines the
average salaries of its members. The American Association of University Professors publishes an annual salary
survey for higher education. The American Federation
of Teachers as well as the National Education Association publish similar surveys for elementary and second-
ary teachers. If you are interested in salaries for engineers, contact the National Society of Professional
Engineers which also conducts its own annual salary
survey. A quick phone call to any professional association should reveal if the organization maintains current
salary information on its members and how you can
access this information. For a complete listing of
professional associations, review either of these two
major directories:

➤ *Encyclopedia of Associations* (Gale Research)

➤ *National Trade and Professional Associations* (Columbia Books)

Most major libraries have current editions of these two directories in their reference section.

3. **Examine federal, state, and local government studies.** Government agencies at all levels periodically conduct wage and salary surveys and publish reports on their findings. Most of these studies are conducted on a regular basis—quarterly, annually, or biannually. Look for the following such surveys and studies:

➤ **U. S. Department of Labor:** The Bureau of Labor Statistics monitors salaries for numerous occupations nationwide. Its findings are published in several quarterly reports for regions and the nation as a whole: *Industry Wage Surveys, Area Wage Surveys, White-Collar Pay,* and *Employee Benefits Survey.* Another publication, the *Monthly Labor Review* which is Bureau's monthly journal, regularly summarizes this statistical information. Many libraries have copies of these reports and the journal, or they can be examined in the Bureau of Labor Statistics regional offices which are located in Boston, New York City, Philadelphia, Atlanta, Chicago, Dallas, Kansas City, San Francisco, and Washington, DC.

➤ **U.S. Office of Personnel Management:** Compiles salary information on government employees at the federal, state, and local levels. The Office of Personnel Management library in Washington, DC will have this information. Also, if you use the Internet, you may check OPM's online site for such information: *www.usajobs.opm.gov*

➤ **Securities and Exchange Commission:** Maintains information on compensation of the nation's top executives. If you're in a high-level executive position which pays in excess of $500,000 a year, be sure to check the SEC's data. It's easily accessed through its online database: *www.sec.gov*

➤ **State and local governments:** Many state and local governments conduct salary and wage surveys for occupations within their geographic area. Contact your state employment commission or county or municipal personnel office to find out if they have such salary information. Your local library also should have information on such surveys. While many of these surveys primarily focus on blue collar occupations within certain industries, some will also include professional and technical positions. While much of this data may be too generalized by industry to be useful in determining salary ranges for particular positions, it will give you some idea of average salaries paid in your particular geographic area.

4. **Contact executive search, employment, and consulting firms:** Many executive search, employment, and consulting firms conduct their own salary surveys

of selected occupations. Some firms are commissioned to do these surveys for corporate clients whereas others compile this information for advertising and public relations purposes. For example, Robert Half International, a job placement firm with over 150 offices nationwide as well as in Canada, the United Kingdom, and Israel, each year publishes the "Robert Half Salary Survey" for positions in accounting, finance, banking, and information systems. Available in booklet form, you can get a free copy of this report by calling any Robert Half office or by visiting their Web site: *www.rhii.com.* Other noted firms conducting salary studies include Source Services (Tel. 1-800-840-8090 or *www.experienceondemand.com*) and Abbott, Langer and Associates (Tel. 708/672-4200 or *www.abbot-langer.com*). While most of these studies are conducted for clients, some are also sold to the general public. While very expensive to acquire ($200 to $500 each in the case of the detailed studies produced by Abbott, Langer, and Associates), some of the salary information appearing in these studies will periodically appear in major magazines and newspapers, such as *Working Woman* and *The Wall Street Journal.*

5. **Review journals and magazines:** Numerous journals and magazines also conduct salary studies as well as publicize the survey findings of other organizations. *Adweek*, for example, publishes an annual salary survey for the advertising field. *Fortune* and *Inc.* magazines usually reveal the salaries of CEOs in Fortune 500 companies. The *Public Relations Journal* publishes salaries of public relations professionals. The January issue of *Working Woman* usually pulls together numerous salary

surveys of associations, employment firms, government, and magazines in its annual salary survey issue. *Compensation Review* keeps compensation specialists informed on salaries and benefits within their industries.

6. **Survey newspapers:** Some newspapers will occasionally conduct their own salary surveys among industries within their community or nationwide. Others report the survey findings of various salary studies. The *National Business Employment Weekly* of the *Wall Street Journal*, for example, periodically conducts nationwide salary surveys and publishes the results in its weekly tabloid of job listings and articles. The results also get reported on the Wall Street Journal's interactive career site: *www.careers.wsj.com.*

7. **Sleuth classified ads and job listings**: Two of the most important sources for salary information are the classified sections of newspapers, magazines, trade journals, and newsletters and the numerous job listings available through employment offices. Many employment ads will reveal the salaries or salary ranges being offered for particular positions. By periodically surveying these ads, you may get a fairly accurate idea of who is paying what in your particular occupation and geographic area.

   Employment offices, both public and private, are repositories for job vacancy announcements and other information on salaries. Employers listing with these offices normally include the salary ranges for each position announced.

   However, don't expect to find salaries listed for all

types of positions. Salaries for blue-collar and hourly positions will most often appear in classified ads and in employment offices. While some ads and vacancy announcements may list the salaries for higher level professional and technical positions, many do not. Invariably they will include general statements such as *"salary and benefits commensurate with qualifications and experience"* or *"we offer a competitive salary and an excellent fringe benefit package."* Alternatively, the ad may request that job seekers submit their salary history, salary requirements, or salary expectations along with their resume when applying for the position. These statements and instructions, in effect, indicate there is flexibility with the salary and thus it is negotiable within certain limits as determined by both the employer and an individual's salary history.

One of the best sources for salary information on professional and technical positions is the *National Business Employment Weekly* of *The Wall Street Journal*. This newspaper includes hundreds of classified ads from all over the country as well as from abroad. Many of the ads will include a specific salary or salary range or notify you they are competitive and that you should submit your salary history. The Sunday editions of major newspapers such as *The New York Times, Washington Post,* and the *Los Angeles Times* will include extensive listings of professional and technical positions. If you survey a few issues of these newspapers, you should be able to get a sense of what employers are offering for your type of position—at least in those specific metropolitan areas. Many of these classified ads are now available on various Web sites of the Internet sponsored by individual newspapers or consortiums of newspapers. If you're Internet savvy, check out the online ads on the two largest employment sites:

Monster Board: *www.monsterboard.com*
CareerPath.com: *www.careerpath.com*

Be sure to survey your own local newspaper and related publications. While newspapers in major metropolitan areas may provide some salary information for positions in major cities, many of these advertisements reflect salaries that are 20 to 30 percent higher than in other communities. Therefore, the classified ads appearing in your local newspaper should more accurately reflect the pricing of jobs in your community. Survey these major national publications, but also know what is being offered locally. At the same time, few ads actually reveal salary information; most request applicants to include their "salary history" or "salary requirements." Consequently, if you have difficulty identifying salaries through these classified ads, try calling a few of the employers and asking about their salary range:

"I'm calling about your ad for a (position) that appeared in today's newspaper. Could you tell me what the salary range is for this position?"

While many employers will not give you this information, or they may say *"it depends on qualifications,"* others will give you their range.

8. **Look for special reports and projects:** You may also discover special reports and projects that include

information on salaries. Faculty and research offices at your local college and university may regularly conduct salary surveys and publish their results in reports that have limited distribution beyond their immediate institution. You may also discover special job search or employment projects that include information on salaries. For example, in our own state of Virginia, a computerized job search program called *Virginia View* includes information on salary ranges both within Virginia and nationwide for numerous types of positions. Centered at Virginia Tech in Blacksburg, Virginia, this program is available throughout the state at most college and university career planning and placement offices as well as in many local libraries and state employment offices. The project also includes a toll-free Career Information Hotline number for state residents in need of job and career assistance: 800/542-5870. You may find similar types of projects operating in your state or local community. Contact your local library, state employment office, or college and university career planning and placement office for information on any such special reports and projects.

Explore the Internet

One of the richest resources for salary information is the Internet. Numerous employment sites include salary information that may prove useful for valuing your worth in today's job market. However, some of the information is misleading. For example, many of the major sites include what they call a "Salary Calculator" which is really a misnomer; it's nothing more than a fancy way of figuring your cost of living in another community as well as advertising online the services of relocation firms. If you want to calculate your new cost of living, go directly to the salary calculator site operated by Home Fair: *homefair.com*. You'll need to go to other Web sites that have actual salary data for specific positions or join online discussion groups or visit a chat room that might be helpful in giving you salary range information for your particular position.

If you are Internet savvy, you should have no problem quickly locating salary information on the Internet. If you start by entering the keywords "Salary Survey" on the various search engines (Alta Vista, Hotbot, InfoSeek, Lycos, Excite, Yahoo), you will get access to 2,000 to 3,000 potential salary resources on the Internet. If you add your job title after "Salary Survey," you'll narrow the number of relevant resources considerably. While many of these sites may be useless, you'll find many others that will be extremely helpful in your search for salary information. In particular, try these sites:

> **The Riley Guide:** We highly recommend starting your Internet research for salary information with "The Riley Guide." This is a key Internet gateway career site maintained by Margaret Dikel (formerly Margaret Riley), an entrepreneurial librarian turned Internet guru specializing in career information. She regularly updates her site with new career resources, many of which deal with salary issues. "The Riley Guide" is currently found at this address:

http://www.dbm.com/jobguide

> **If you are Internet savvy, you should have no problem quickly locating salary information on the Internet.**

The section on "What Am I Worth?" will take you into the latest Internet resources dealing with salary issues.

➤ **Jobsmart:** Initially designed as an online career library resource for California (Sacramento, Los Angeles, and the San Francisco Bay Area), this site provides direct linkages to more than 150 salary surveys which are classified by various occupational fields:

http://jobsmart.org/tools/salary/index.htm

In fact, this may be the only Internet site you need to visit to find the salary information you need!

➤ **American Compensation Association:** This professional organization sponsors numerous compensation studies, hosts conferences, publishes journals and newsletters, and offers a variety of services relating to compensation issues and trends. Their Web site provides synopses of recent articles on compensation trends: *www.acaonline.org*

➤ **Employee Benefits Research Institute:** This employee benefits think tank provides a great deal of online information on benefit trends under its "Special Fact Sheets" and "What's New" sections. A recent fact cited included employers' average cost of health insurance per employee in 1996: $4,332.00. See: *www.ebri.org*

➤ **Wageweb:** This is an online salary survey system which includes salary surveys on more than 150 positions, such as HR, administrative, finance, information management, engineering, health care, sales/marketing, and manufacturing. Serious users—primarily employers—pay a $100 a year membership fee for unlimited access to this database. This is a real bargain considering the fact that many salary surveys can cost from $200 to $500 per position if purchased in paper report form. Wageweb's Internet address is:

http://www.wageweb.com

Many of the major Internet career sites may also have information on salaries that go beyond the "Salary Calculator" misnomer. The information may be in the form of job listings and salary surveys, or you may uncover this information in chat groups and discussion forums. You can do your own quick salary survey by posing some form of this question in a chat group:

"I'm doing an informal survey of salaries for _____. Do you know what the salary range for this type of position would be in your company or area?"

This question will most likely elicit several responses which may prove useful. However, keep in mind that such responses may or may not be accurate representations since they are based upon opinions or a few observations rather than upon systematic research. You really know little about the source of this data.

If you haven't done so, you should familiarize yourself with these major Internet sites that specialize on jobs and careers:

➤ **America's Job Bank:** *www.ajb.dni.us*. Operated by the U.S. Department of Labor, this is the closest thing to a comprehensive nationwide computerized job bank. Linked to state employment offices, which daily post thousands of new job listings filed by employers with their offices, individuals should soon be able to explore more than a million job vacancies in both the public and private sectors at any time through this service. While the jobs listing cover everything from entry-level to professional and managerial positions, expect to find a disproportionate number of jobs requiring less than a college education listed in this job bank. This service is also available at state employment offices as well as at other locations (look for touch screen kiosks in shopping centers and other public places) which are set up for public use.

➤ **CareerCity:** *www.careercity.com.* Operated by one of the major publishers of career books and CD-ROMs (Adams Media), this online service includes job listings, discussion forums (conferences, workshops, Q&A sessions), specialized career services, and publications.

➤ **CareerMosaic:** *www.careermosaic.com.* This job service is appropriate for college students and professionals. Includes hundreds of job listings in a large variety of fields, from high-tech to retail, with useful information on each employer and job. Includes a useful feature whereby college students can communicate directly with employers (e-mail) for information and advice—a good opportunity to do "inside" networking. Includes a "Wage & Salary Information" section that has linkages to several salary surveys:

www.careermosaic.com/cm/crc/crc18.html.

➤ **CareerPath:** *www.careerpath.com.* This is the one-stop-shop for classified job listings from 31 major newspapers across the country. Includes over 400,000 job listings each month. Updated daily.

➤ **CareerWeb:** *www.careerweb.com.* Operated by Land-
mark Communications which also publishes several newspapers and operates The Weather Channel, The Travel
Channel, and InfiNet, this service is a major recruitment
source for hundreds of companies nationwide. Free service
for job seekers who can explore hundreds of job listings,
many of which are in high-tech fields. Includes company
profile pages to learn about a specific company. Also
operates a popular companion site for transitioning military personnel:

www.greentogray.com or *www.bluetogray.com*

Occasionally runs useful articles on salary negotiations. A
quality operation.

➤ **E-Span:** *www.espan.com.* This full-service online employment resource includes thousands of job listings in a
variety of fields as well as operates a huge database of
resumes. Job seekers can send their resumes to be included
in their database of job listings and search for appropriate
job openings through the Interactive Employment Network. Also includes useful career information and resources, including linkages to Source Service's (*www.
experienceondemand.com*) salary surveys.

➤ **JobTrak:** *www.jobtrak.com.* This organization posts over
500 new job openings each day from companies seeking
college students and graduates. Includes company profiles,
job hunting tips, and employment information. Good
source for entry-level positions, including both full-time
and part-time positions, and for researching companies.

➤ **JobWeb:** *www.jobweb.org*. Operated by the National Association of Colleges and Employers (NACE), this service is designed to do everything: compiles information on employers, including salary surveys; lists job openings; provides job search assistance; and maintains a resume database.

▪ **The Monster Board**: *www.monster.com*. This site provides job seekers with three primary services—job search, on-line resume building, and employer profiles. The job search provides for intelligent querying of both a U.S. and international job database. The U.S. database contains over 16,500 job opportunities. *The Employer Profiles* contains information on over 4,000 corporations worldwide.

▪ **Online Career Center:** *www.occ.com*. This is the grandaddy of career centers on the Web. It's basically a resume database and job search service. Individuals send their resume (free if transmitted electronically) which is then included in the database. They also can search for appropriate job openings. Employers pay for using the service.

Conduct Your Own Salary Survey

One of the quickest ways to gather relatively accurate information on salary ranges in your community or region is to conduct your own salary survey through a combination of networking through your connections or making cold calls to those who have useful information. You can easily do this in a few hours by contacting the following individuals and groups which should yield a great deal of useful salary information relevant to your position:

➤ **Friends and colleagues:** Contact friends or colleagues who might be in similar positions as you and ask them if they have any idea what the "going rate" is for someone with your skills and experience. Your opener might go something like this:

> *"Hi Ken. I need some help. I'm in the process of conducting an informal salary survey. Would you know, or do you know someone who might know, what the current salary range is for someone with five years experience as a speech-language pathologist working in a private clinic?"*

This question should elicit useful information or referrals to others who might have similar information. Be sure to ask for referrals regardless of whether your friend or colleague gives you useful salary range information:

> *"Who else might have similar information on such salary ranges? Can you think of two or three other people I might contact?"*

Make sure you confine your questioning to friends and colleagues *outside* your current place of employment. If you start asking this question with current employees, the word may get out that you are snooping around about peoples' salaries which could be grounds for your dismissal!

➤ **Employment specialists:** Call your state or local employment office, or a career counselor at your local community college or university, and ask them a similar question: *"Do you know, or would you know anyone who might know, what the current salary range is for . . ."*

➤ **Headhunters:** Most representatives of executive search firms, or headhunters, keep abreast of current salary ranges for a variety of occupational fields and positions. Since headhunters work for employers, they are very familiar with the going market rate for salaries. You may discover that headhunters are your best source for salary information simply because they are constantly in the market dealing with candidates, employers, and salaries. If you don't know any headhunters, consult the annual "bible" in this business: *Directory of Executive Search Firms* (Kennedy Information). It includes the names, addresses, and phone numbers of more than 4,000 executive search firms. Keep in mind that most headhunters focus on positions that pay in excess of $50,000 a year. They are especially knowledgeable about positions paying in the $70,000 to $150,000 range.

> The most useful salary information will come from your networking activities with fellow professionals who know the current market value of your position.

➤ **Other sources:** Again, don't forget to talk with your local librarian, contact local resources (try your Chamber of Commerce, minister, or insurance agent), call professional associations, or go online to network for salary information. You'll be surprised how easy it is to get good information on a subject that is usually not talked about much in employment circles.

The best quality and most useful salary information will most likely come from your networking activities with fellow professionals who know the current market value of your position as well as someone with your particular skills and experience. Keep in mind that the market value for your position may not be the same as the market value for your skills and experience. If, as we mentioned earlier, your position does not accurately reflect your day-to-day work, you may need to concentrate on assessing the value of your skills and experience and then relating them to a promotion to another position that more accurately reflects the value of your work.

Set Your Salary Goals

Once you've gathered your salary information and have a very good idea of what you're really worth in today's job market, you should turn your attention to setting your new salary goal. Complete the following items:

1. My current compensation package is worth $_____.

2. Based on my research of salary comparables, my current compensation package would be worth $_____ to $ _____ with other employers in this area.

3. The difference between what I'm currently getting and what I should be getting is approximately $ _____.

4. Based on what I know I'm worth with other employers and what I believe I should be worth to my current employer, I will present a salary proposal to my boss that increases my total compensation package by $ _____ which represents a _____% increase in compensation this year.

5. My new compensation package should include the following increases and/or additions:

➤ Salary: $ _____

➤ Benefits: _____

_____

_____

_____

_____

➤ Perks: _____

_____

_____

_____

_____

6. If my boss does not give me what I believe I'm worth, I'm prepared to do the following:

❑ Resign and look for another job

❑ Accept what I'm offered

❑ Reach a compromise

❑ Develop creative options

Whatever you do, make sure you have a clear idea of what it is you want to result from the upcoming meeting with your boss (your salary goal) as well as what you plan to do if you are not satisfied with the outcome of your meeting. You need to consider your options which we will address in the next chapter as the third step to salary success.

7

Consider Your Options

S o what are you going to do once you're armed with lots of good data on your worth and you've set your salary goals? Are you ready to see your boss about a raise or do you need to do some other things before the big meeting? Your next step should be to consider your options which are essentially two-fold: remaining on-the-job versus changing employers. These options lay the ground work for developing a winning strategy for talking money to power.

On-the-Job Options

Let's assume you enjoy your job and the people you work with. Like most employees, you would prefer staying with your current employer rather than look for another job—as long as the cash, benefits, and perks are right. But you're also realistic, especially after you've done your salary research you've learned your compensation package is not up to par. The cash, benefits, and perks may not be what you expected, but you still prefer working for your current employer. After all, there are numerous costs and risks involved in changing employers. So what can you do with your current employer to ensure that your compensation expectations are met?

Let's assume you prepare a well-reasoned case for a 13 percent salary increase. You've done your research on salary comparables and know you are worth from 10 to 15 percent more than you are currently paid. You've also discovered that other elements in your compensation package appear below the norm for your type of position—health and life insurance coverage, dental plan, vacation days, and employer contribution to a 401(k) plan. You can cite concrete examples of your performance that have contributed to the increased profitability of the firm. Indeed, you believe you are presenting an extremely strong case for receiving a significant salary increase. How could your employer not agree that you are worth 13 percent more than you are currently receiving?

> **Few employees are indispensable to a company; most are replaceable and often at a lower salary rate.**

It's always best to expect the unexpected. While you should go for optimal outcomes, always anticipate worst case scenarios. Remember, few employees are indispensable to a company; most are replaceable and often at a lower salary rate. As you get older and reach the higher end of an employer's salary scale, you may have less and less room to negotiate a higher salary simply because you are beginning to cost the company more than someone who is younger and has lower salary requirements.

Regardless of how well documented and reasoned a case you present for a raise, there's a chance the outcome of your meeting with the boss may be less than satisfactory. After all, you are not the only employee the company must consider for increased compensation. Your new salary expectations may exceed the employer's norm. And he may be convinced, whether realistic or not, that he will be able to replace you with "new blood" whose salary demands will be less than your new requirements. He likes you and your work, but isn't able to accept your salary requirements. Indeed, he may present you with a "take it or leave it" decision that has already been made prior to your meeting and persuasive presentation. He may not play the "everything is negotiable game" since he knows he really doesn't have to negotiate with you. He's in the driver's seat. But you could cost the company a lot if you leave, simply because of the high costs of recruiting and training a replacement.

So what do you plan to do if this worst case "take it or leave it" scenario is presented to you? Are you prepared to leave or will you decide to stay under the "take it" terms presented by your employer? If you plan to stay, consider the following options that may still move you closer to your compensation goals:

1. **Consider what it will cost both you and your employer if you leave.** Changing employers involves certain risks and costs for both you and your employer. For you, it means job hunting costs, retraining costs, risk costs, stress costs, and perhaps relocation costs. A new job always involves a certain element of risk—you may not work out during the first 90 days and thus you find yourself unemployed. At the same time, it will probably be more costly for the employer to lose you. Many employers figure replacing an employee will cost them anywhere from $10,000 to $50,000, depending on the position—and more for executive-level positions that have severance provisions in the employment contract. In fact, many employers routinely figure replacement costs at 100-200% of the former employee's base salary! These costs are incurred in four major areas: opportunity costs, productivity costs, recruitment costs, and training costs. It

takes time and money to get a new employee up and running to an expected level of performance. An unhappy employee, one whose compensation expectations are not met, also costs a company in terms of opportunities and productivity. If you are currently making $50,000 a year, expect your costs of leaving and acquiring a new job to be around $10,000; expect the employer's cost of your quitting to be closer to $50,000. Knowing this, an employer would be wise to listen to you and reach common ground on your compensation requirements. For to do otherwise would probably be

> **Many employers routinely figure replacement costs at 100-200% of the former employee's base salary!**

"pennywise but pound foolish" on the part of the employer who may literally not know his soon to be incurred replacement costs!

2. **Focus on benefits and perks rather than on cash alone.** Benefits and perks do translate into real cash, especially if they consist of tax-free or tax-deferred compensation or equity in the company. Benefits and perks may be less costly to the company but they may translate into a significant increase in compensation for you. Consequently, by focusing on benefits and perks, you may be dealing with a classic "win-win" scenario for both you and the employer.

3. **Consider higher incentive compensation, from bonuses to variable pay.** Here's the ultimate "win-win" option. It follows one of the major trends in compensation today—offering conservative base pay but providing greater incentive compensation. If your current compensation package, for example, tends to be heavily weighted on base salary

and standard benefits, you may want to focus on "incen-tivizing" your compensation. This approach especially appeals to employers who prefer shifting pay-and-perfor-mance risks to employees by providing them with addi-tional compensation, if and when they achieve or exceed specific goals. It also means such compensation will not continue to inflate the organization's base pay since it is a variable form of payment—it varies with the performance of the company, team, or individual. Consequently, if your new base salary requirements are unacceptable to your boss, discuss an incentivized bonus option that can be structured around specific performance indicators, such as a 2 percent commission, equity (discounted stock purchase), or an annual or discretionary cash bonus for all new business you generate beyond what is considered to be the expected norm. Think in terms of how you could best incentivize your work with specific performance indicators that go beyond the expected. In fact, you may want to skip base salary altogether and begin shifting your compensation to a more performance-oriented variable pay program. In effect, you've created an offer that's hard to refuse—potentially a "no-risk-all-reward" option for the employer.

4. **Discuss the possibility of scheduling a salary review meeting in another three months.** Rethink the purpose of your current meeting. If you can't reach agreement and you're not willing to quit, try to keep the compensation issue open by redefining the purpose of the meeting—consider this to be a preliminary meeting to a formal salary review meeting. Try to schedule this next meeting within three months with your performance being the central issue on the agenda. In the meantime, think how you can best incentivize your future compensation.

5. **Choose an appropriate language to frame your questions and requests.** Your choice of language will influence the outcome of negotiations and set the stage for future negotiations. Aggressive or assertive demand-oriented language may be too intimidating to individuals who believe they are in the driver's seat or for those who need to be persuaded to become more responsive to your needs. When talking about money, a less assertive and more probing approach that uses possibility-oriented language may be most effective. If you frame your requests in the question form, *"Is it possible to...?"*, you may find

> **Use possibility-oriented language to frame your compensation requests.**

your boss to be much more receptive to your salary requirements. For example, assuming you are the boss, how would you respond to these three statements?

"I want a 13 percent salary increase this year."

"I feel I deserve a 13 percent salary increase this year."

"Is it possible for us to do a 13 percent increase this year?"

The first two statements may elicit a quick acceptance or rejection while the third possibility-oriented question may better enable both of you to reach some form of mutual agreement if you have been able to demonstrate your value. After all, anything is possible—if you think about it and work toward a solution!

6. **Explore the possibility of a promotion.** Salary ranges are usually tied to specific positions. If your new salary requirements appear to exceed the salary range specified for your current position, you need to focus on the possibility of being promoted to a new position in which the salary range exceeds your current salary. A promotion also might mean creating a new position with a new salary range. When you focus on the possibility of receiving a promotion, you begin thinking outside the box (your current position) and thus provide your boss with an additional rationale for giving you a raise.

Changing Employers

Many people change jobs every three to seven years. They do so due to a variety of "push" and "pull" factors: their career quickly plateaus within an organization; they seek better opportunities elsewhere; they are unhappy with their work and/or the people they work with; they become victims of downsizing; they get fired; or they decide to relocate to a new city or state. One other important reason is that they are attracted to the salary, benefits, and perks of other employers.

If you are unhappy with your current job and its attendant salary, benefits, and perks, you should consider looking for another job that is more compatible with your employment requirements. However, before you do so, remember there are certain costs involved in making such a move. Assess your current situation by responding to the following statements. Circle the response that most accurately reflects your situation and then calculate a composite score that indicates whether or not you should or should not begin looking for another job:

	Yes				No
1. My future looks very good with my current employer.	5	4	3	2	1
2. My employer usually listens to my ideas and responds accordingly.	5	4	3	2	1
3. My employer will most likely respond positively to my ideas on incentivizing my compensation.	5	4	3	2	1
4. I enjoy working with my co-workers.	5	4	3	2	1
5. I'm respected by my boss, co-workers, and clients.	5	4	3	2	1
6. I look forward to going to work every Monday.	5	4	3	2	1
7. My family is happy with my current employment situation.	5	4	3	2	1
8. I have very few complaints about my employer and job.	5	4	3	2	1
9. I'm recognized by my employer as someone who is very valuable to the organization and who would be missed if I left.	5	4	3	2	1
10. If I could change my current job, my employer would most likely help me redesign my job or work toward a promotion.	5	4	3	2	1

11. With my current employer, I feel
    I'm learning a great deal and
    improving my skills for the future.   5   4   3   2   1

12. I really love my job and the lifestyle
    it allows me to pursue.   5   4   3   2   1

                          TOTAL

If your total score is 50 points or higher, chances are you are a good candidate for staying with your current employer and "working things out" in the compensation and promotion departments. You may be foolish to jump ship for another employer that may or may not be as good as your current employer.

However, should your score fall below 35 points, this might be a good time to do a complete career checkup to make sure you are doing what you really enjoy doing and that you are advancing your career in the desired direction. It may be time to start "testing the waters" to see what other employers have to offer. By focusing on this third step in the 10-step process to getting a raise, you may decide it's really time to seriously reassess your current employment situation and develop a well thought-out plan to transition to another more responsive employer. Changing employers and jobs may be just what you and your career need at this time!

Consider Other Options

You might be able to think of some other options prior to having a salary meeting with your boss. Two in particular come to mind when considering staying or leaving:

1. **Try redesigning your job**. When you do research on salary comparables, one of the biggest problems is whether or not you are comparing apples to apples or apples to oranges. The tendency is to compare job titles rather than job functions. For example, the job of a Financial Analyst in Company X may be very different from a Financial Analyst in Company Y. The differences in compensation may reflect real differences in levels of responsibility and specific duties and functions rather than evidence of inequities between positions. To only compare job titles is to fundamentally misunderstand the nature of compensation. Only after you have had a chance to examine the day-to-day realities of job functions and performance do you really get a clear picture of job, and salary, comparables. Knowing this, you may want to consider redesigning your job so that it is more in line with the norm or more comparable with your particular strengths and goals. In the process of doing this, you may be creating a new job for yourself within the company—one that deserves higher compensation.

   > To only compare job titles is to fundamentally misunderstand the nature of compensation.

2. **Consider putting yourself on the job market 24 hours a day, 7 days a week**. The continuing movement of the job market from paper postings to an electronic format on the Internet with integrated employment sites offering job listings, resume databases, and employer profiles means you can literally stay in the job market the rest of your life rather than re-enter and exit the job market every three to seven years! If you periodically explore the more than 3,000

employment sites on the Internet, as well as enter your resume in some of the key databases, you will stay connected to the job market. We highly recommend staying in contact with the major sites, especially those we identified in Chapter 6 (America's Job Bank, CareerCity, Career Path, Career Mosaic, CareerWeb, E-Span, Job Trak, The Monster Board, and the Online Career Center) as well as sites that specialize in your specific occupational area. Some of these sites will be operated by professional associations related to your occupational field. You'll learn a great deal about who's hiring whom and for how much. You'll learn more and more about the evolution of compensation packages and sample current demands for your particular mix of experience and skills. Best of all, you will be well positioned to make a move to another employer, if and when that time seems appropriate. No longer will you have to get yourself "up to speed" to re-enter the job market when the time comes to seek new employment. Taking care of your career means keeping your resume updated as well as periodically exploring the many employment opportunities listed on various Internet job sites. By so doing, you will keep up with today's rapidly changing job market. You'll have a better idea of what you're really worth, what skills you need to have, and how difficult it will be for you to find another job that is better than your current one.

Negotiating From Strength

Negotiating compensation in today's employment environment is really all about options. The more options you bring to the table, the higher the probability you will walk away a winner. And if those options are initially low cost and low risk for your employer (i.e., do not result in a major increase in base salary), chances are you will both walk away with having negotiated a win-win compensation package that will soon be very beneficial to you, your employer, and your company. It simply doesn't get any better than this for your long-term career development!

8

Develop a Strategy For Talking Money to Power

Assuming your know your boss well, your next step is to develop a strategy that will persuade your boss to give you a raise. This means analyzing and understanding your boss's habits and decision-making style. How does she, for example, like to deal with personnel issues? Does she normally schedule a formal meeting, deal with such issues informally, or prefer avoiding such issues altogether? Is Monday usually a bad day to meet? What about Friday afternoon? Does your boss usually take the lead in discussing such issues or is she a good listener who expects you to do most of the talking?

Analyze Your Boss

Developing a strategy first of all involves understanding your boss and then developing a strategy that best responds to her behavior. You no doubt already know a lot about your boss's behavior. After

120

all, you see her regularly and thus should know her behavior vis-a-vis you and others. Begin analyzing her behavior by asking yourself these questions:

1. How does my boss usually deal with important personnel issues?

2. What day of the week, time of the day, or in what situation does my boss seem to be most responsive to my ideas?

3. When we last talked about a raise, how did she deal with the issue? Who initiated the meeting and conversation.

4. What did I do that may have made her respond the way she did?

5. How flexible is she in dealing with important issues?

6. When dealing with important issues, does she often seek common ground, negotiate, and compromise?

7. When was I most effective with my boss? What did I do that made her so receptive to my ideas?

8. What types of objections does she usually raise to me as well as to compensation issues?

9. Does my boss have the authority to make decisions concerning raises or must she talk to management first?

10. How has my boss evaluated my performance this year?

11. Does she genuinely respect me professionally as well as like me personally?

12. Can I talk frankly with her about my work, my compensation, and my future with the company without fear that these subjects will be held against me?

13. Does she respond well to organized presentations of others or does she prefer to be in control of the agenda and sequence of the presentation?

14. What's the probability that she will have a positive response to my compensation request?

15. Will this meeting improve my relationship with my boss or might it actually damage my relationship?

Once you've considered these 15 questions, as well as other questions you generate specific to your situation, you should have a good idea as to how best to approach your boss about the compensation issue. You should have a sense of what might or might not work with your boss. For example, is it best to give a formal presentation to your boss about your compensation research results requirements or would it be better to ask a series of leading questions that gets your boss to talk about the compensation issue? The most savvy salary negotiators understand their bosses and approach them with appropriate strategies.

Outline a Briefings Approach

What are you going to do when you meet with your boss about a raise? Assuming you meet in her office, are you just going to sit in front of her desk nervously and wait for her to initiate the conversation or will you take the initiative in presenting your case for a raise? We recommend the latter—a proactive approach that consists of a well thought-out presentation that focuses on why you should be given a raise. This presentation, which is actually a one-on-one briefing, is designed to persuade. As such, it must be rich in **supports** which normally consist of examples, statistics, comparisons, contrasts, testimonials, and stories.

If you know your bosses' habits and decision-making style, you should be able to approach him or her with a high probability of success. We strongly recommend approaching your boss as if you were developing a presentation in which your goal is to persuade the listener to agree with your proposition. The following elements of preparation should go into your persuasive briefing:

1. Determine your goal (Chapter 5)

2. Analyze your audience (your boss and anyone to whom she will need to present your case) (Chapters 5 and 8)

3. Consider the situation or setting (Chapter 10)

4. Gather information (Chapter 5)

5. Limit your time (Chapter 11)

6. Limit your focus (Chapter 11)

7. Determine your main points (Chapter 11)

8. Compile supports (Chapter 6)

9. Organize ideas for easy understanding (Chapter 11)

10. Provide listener with a statement of reasons (Chapter 6)

After you've prepared in this manner, begin developing the actual presentation by incorporating these key elements:

1. Control your nervousness (Chapter 10)
2. Develop an attention-getting introduction (Chapter 10)
3. Focus on your "Perfect Salary Pitch" (Chapter 11)
4. Anticipate and respond to objections (Chapter 12)
5. Summarize and close for further action (Chapter 13)

Be Your Best Self

Under no circumstances should you attempt to script this meeting by memorizing exactly what you plan to say. If you attempt to do so, you'll most likely exhibit nervousness, forget your lines, and sound insincere with what will most likely appear to be a canned and lifeless presentation. Your strategy should consist of notes of the points you want to make. While the briefing should be well organized, it also should sound extemporaneous and exhibit two qualities most employers like to see in their employees—enthusiasm and sincerity.

9

Schedule a Timely Meeting

Timing is everything! That's never more true than when you schedule a meeting to discuss compensation with your boss. When's the best time to schedule a meeting? How do you approach your boss? What exactly should you say? Where should you meet? What do you do if he wants to meet right now and in his office? What should you do if the timing unexpectedly goes bad?

Take Control, If You Can

You may or may not have much control over the timing of this meeting since you will most likely have to fit your schedule into the boss's schedule, or the salary meeting may already be pre-scheduled as part of an annual salary review. Nonetheless, you should try to affect both the timing and the setting of the meeting, or at least make sure you have plenty of time to prepare for this meeting. Ideally, you should complete your first eight steps of the

125

10 steps to salary success prior to scheduling this meeting.

There are several things you can do to affect both the scheduling and outcomes of this meeting. Make sure you don't prematurely schedule this meeting before you've had time to do your necessary preparation. You must put together a dynamite salary presentation for this critical meeting that will most likely affect your future earnings for years to come.

Affect the Annual Salary Review

Whether you have an annual or semi-annual salary review coming up soon or if you must seize the initiative and request a meeting with your boss, make sure you give yourself plenty of time to put together your presentation. If this meeting is scheduled by your boss, chances are he already has an agenda and presentation planned. In many cases, the formal annual salary review meeting is designed to communicate management's evaluation of your performance and inform you what your raise will be. If this decision has already been made from top down, you may have feel you little input into this process and the salary decision. But even in this instance, if what you are offered seems low based on your preparation, you should be able to present your salary comparables and stress your performance. On the other hand, this meeting could be conducted as a give-and-take session in which the employer discusses your performance with you, including various compensation issues which have yet to be finalized. Try to structure the situation according to the points discussed in Chapter 10, communicate your "Perfect Salary Pitch"

> Make sure you don't prematurely schedule this meeting before you've had time to do your necessary preparation.

as outlined in Chapter 11, and anticipate the objections presented in Chapter 12. If you do this, you should have a major input into the decision-making process. You'll be salary savvy in a situation that is normally controlled by the employer and communicated top-down to the employee.

Select the Perfect Time

If you have taken the initiative to request a meeting with your boss, you have greater control over situational constraints. There may not be any perfect times to schedule a salary review meeting, but there are definitely bad times to have this meeting. You don't want to schedule a meeting at these unfortunate times:

- the value of the company's stock just plunged by 10 percentage points

- the quarterly report just came in and profits are down by 35 percent for the quarter

- management just decided to layoff 5 percent of the workforce

- the department is under a tight deadline to get a report out within the next 10 days

- your boss is in the midst of a nasty divorce and next week he has a day in court

- your boss's mother died

- your boss just fired one of the more outspoken employees

- your department is facing some major cutbacks because of over staffing and inefficiencies

- the U.S. Department of Labor just released its new unemployment figures for the month—unemployment is up to 8 percent in what now appears to be an employer's market

- economists announce that the current rate of inflation (.03 percent) is the lowest rate in over 50 years and the average salary increase this past year was only 2 percent

> **The perfect time for your meeting is when your boss is in a positive, upbeat mood about the four key ingredients that determine increased compensation: the company, himself, his subordinates, and you.**

Sometimes you may be aware of these bad times but many times they come as complete surprises—the ubiquitous "unfortunate timing" episode.

So what is a perfect time for this meeting? The perfect time is when your boss is in a positive, upbeat mood about the four key ingredients that determine increased compensation: the company, himself, his subordinates, and you. The company is more profitable than ever, and he's pleased with his work and the work of his subordinates. Performance is considered excellent and resources abound. In other words, your boss is feeling very positive about the present and future. Best of all, you're seen as someone who is really contributing to this positive state of affairs. Given this upbeat atmosphere, chances are your boss is in a very generous mood; he has the right attitude for your meeting. He wants to continue feeling good about the company, his employees, and you.

If you work in such a profitable company, it would be to your advantage to monitor the company's progress. If you know the company or your division will be showing strong profits for the quarter, try to schedule your meeting immediately following the announcement of the quarterly figures. However, if you suspect profits will be down for the next quarter, try to get your meeting in before the announcement of the bad news. Good news for the company will most likely translate into good news for you, but only if you schedule your salary meeting around the time the good news is announced.

Another good time to schedule this meeting is right after one of your major accomplishments has been communicated to your boss. For example, you may have just saved the company $50,000 by instituting a new competitive bidding process; you brought in a new client who will be doing $300,000 in new business with your company; your proposal just landed a $1 million contract for the company; or your published research findings in the New England Journal of Medicine gave your company excellent publicity in both the print and electronic media. Any of these "special events" are optimal times to schedule a salary meeting with your boss.

Other optimal times relate to the ebb and flow of work. Try, for example, scheduling the meeting during a time in which your boss is least under stress or preoccupied with other activities. This might be a Tuesday or Thursday (Mondays and Fridays may be especially hectic days); the first thing in the morning; immediately following lunch; or the last meeting of the day. Try to avoid squeezing your meeting between other more important meetings. Otherwise, your meeting may appear insignificant in comparison to these other more demanding meetings. Indeed, your boss may have difficulty giving you his full attention since he may be mentally preoccupied thinking about the last meeting or planning for the next meeting. You want his full attention.

When scheduling this meeting, keep the following considerations in mind:

❑ Company's financial situation
❑ Boss's attitude and mood
❑ Productivity of your work group
❑ Current visibility of your work
❑ On-going activities and competing meetings
❑ Time of day
❑ Day of the week

If you keep these timing elements in mind when you schedule your salary meeting, you should be able to select a good time that gives you the greatest advantage in presenting your case for a raise.

Give Yourself Enough Time

We strongly recommend planning for this meeting *before* scheduling the meeting with your boss. After all, your request may result in an immediate meeting! However, if you've not prepared for your meeting according to our ten steps, be sure to give yourself at least seven days to prepare. If, for example, you see your boss on Monday, ask if you could have a meeting sometime next week. You need not announce that this is a salary review meeting—a meeting "about my work" is sufficient. In the process of discussing your work you, of course, will focus on the issue of compensation. You might say something like this:

"I would like to get together with you soon concerning my work. Would it be possible for us to meet sometime next week?"

If he responds by recommending an earlier date, such as sometime in the next three days, respond by saying something like this:

"Next week would really work better for me since I need some time to pull together information for the meeting. Would that be possible?"

If he probes, or indicates he can meet immediately, he might say:

"What's on your mind? Is it something we can talk about now or sometime later today or tomorrow? I have free time this afternoon."

Avoid this tempting offer, unless you are very well prepared to proceed according to your 10 steps. You might respond by adding the following information concerning your agenda:

"Next week really would be better. I want to talk to you about my performance and my future with the company. I would also like to review my current compensation package. I have a few questions in this area."

By saying this, you put your boss on notice that you consider this to be a very important meeting since you are in the process of compiling information for presentation. You revealed in general terms the nature of your agenda.

> **By scheduling the meeting several days in advance, you put your boss on notice that you consider this to be a very important meeting.**

Whatever you do, don't schedule this meeting before its time. If you want to be most effective, you simply must get your act together in the form of a powerful presentation that clearly communicates to your boss why you believe you are worth more than you are currently receiving. In fact, if you believe events might take over and force a meeting before you are prepared, you will be much better off preparing first and then scheduling the meeting. After all, this meeting is too important, and the financial stakes too high, to be left to chance timing.

When Timing in Not So Perfect

Regardless of how hard you try to pick an optimal time, sometimes unexpected events occur that turn what was ostensibly good timing into bad timing. For example, the day before your scheduled meeting, a production crisis occurs in your office and your boss is most unhappy; the government unexpectedly releases its new unemployment, inflation, and income figures which actually weaken your case; or your boss has just learned she has cancer on the same day she was in an automobile accident with an uninsured motorist. This are bad times to be discussing a salary increase. If anything like this happens during the period just before your scheduled meeting, try to reschedule the meeting at a more appropriate, and hopefully more positive, time. Ask your boss the following:

> *"Would it be possible to reschedule tomorrow's meeting? I need a little more time. How would next week work for you?"*

Whatever you do, avoid bad timing. You'll know it when you see it—it will speak to you as follows: "This is no longer a good time to be talking about money with my boss who probably is not in a position to be open-minded and generous." Your compensation is too important to be left to the whims of bad timing that may negatively affect your boss's attitude and mood toward both you and your salary.

10

Structure the Situation

Your situation will consist of the setting and the agenda for the meeting. You can assume the setting will most likely be your boss's office, something you have little control over beyond the seating arrangement. The agenda, however, is something you can affect to a very large degree. Indeed, it is to your benefit to largely control the agenda by creating what we call the "one-page talking paper" that focuses attention on the key points in your presentation.

Affect the Setting, If You Can

It would be to your advantage to hold the salary meeting in your office, especially since you may have supporting materials in your files or on your computer that would strengthen your presentation. If, for example, you have a database or Web sites you wish to demonstrate from your computer, you would have the perfect excuse to meet in your office. When you hold the meeting in your office, you have the extra edge of being in more control of your setting. You're in an environment that can best demonstrate your work. When selecting alternative settings, you might ask your boss the following question:

"Would it be okay if we meet in my office? I have some things I would like to show you on my computer."

Chances are this question will result in moving the meeting to your office or work area where you will be more relaxed and in control of your environment; you also may be surrounded by photos of your family, which add an important personal element to this setting (the photos may remind the boss that her decisions affect a family, not just you the individual). Be sure your work environment appears well organized and efficient. You'll sit at the command and control area of the desk and in the best chair; your boss will most likely sit in a chair normally reserved for subordinates or outsiders. This arrangement may give you some psychological advantage during the meeting. Indeed, you may feel more confident talking about yourself and your compensation from such an employee-friendly environment.

> **Be sure your work environment appears well organized and efficient. Personalize your setting with family photos—those the boss also helps support!**

However, corporate etiquette favors having the salary review meeting in the boss's office. The compensation issue falls within her authority and thus the meeting normally takes place within her work environment. She, too, may have documents (your personnel file) she needs to quickly access in her office files or on her computer. If the boss's work environment feels intimidating—a big window, lots of office space and furniture, frequent interruptions from the outside—try to focus on your message rather than on your surroundings.

Structure the Agenda

You need to bring structure to this meeting. Indeed, he who structures the agenda will most likely have the most influence on the outcomes of this meeting. The agenda specifies the logical flow of key points you wish to emphasize, from beginning to end. The agenda is something you prepare ahead of time and commit to memory or jot down on a notecard or piece of paper. These are points you wish to emphasize or the message you wish to convey during your meeting. It's essentially an outline of your briefing or presentation. Your agenda might look something like this:

> **He who structures the agenda will most likely have the most influence on the outcomes of this meeting.**

1. Purpose of meeting
2. Presentation of accomplishments
3. Changes in current position and job, if any
4. Research findings on comparable positions
5. Current compensation package
6. Goals for next year
7. Proposed compensation package
8. Summary and close

Your presentation should unfold in a very logical, step-by-step manner that continuously stresses your value to the employer:

1. **Purpose of meeting:** How you open this meeting will set the tone for the final outcome. Avoid jumping right into the meat of the matter—money. You need to establish good rapport. Remember, the more your boss likes you, the more difficult it may be to say "no" to you. Make the personal connection along with the professional connection; let her know you really like working with her. If you're meeting in your office and your family photo is in the background as you talk, you may be subtly emphasizing that your whole family likes working here. Your opening comments might include some small talk about what you're currently working on and how committed you are to your work and the company. Talk about "we" as a team. For example,

> **The more your boss likes you, the more difficult it may be to say "no" to you.**

> *"I've been working on the Fireside account these past two months. If all goes well in their meeting today, **we** may soon be doing major business with them. **We** should sign a contract within the next three weeks. This one has been a real challenge, but one that really improved **our** ability to compete with Dynet Associates. I think **we** will be seeing some major contract work coming our way in the months ahead. I'm also really excited about the proposal **we** have with Cellular Systems."*

From here the small talk should transition to the purpose of the meeting. Start by establishing a close connection between you and your boss which, in effect, creates common ground for focusing on the real purpose of the meeting—a raise or promotion:

> *"Thanks so much for meeting with me about my work. As you know, I've been very happy working with you, the team, and the company. I've learned a great deal and believe I've contributed substantially to the growth of our company. Zitra is like family to me. You've always been very supportive of my work and have given me invaluable feedback on how I can best improve my work. I really appreciate all you have done to ensure that I continue to grow in my career here at Zitra."*

Now transition to the real purpose of the meeting:

> *"It's been nearly a year since we had a chance to discuss my performance and review my compensation package. I would like go over several things with you including what I've been doing this past year, how my position has evolved, and where I stand in relationship to others in my profession. I've had some time to pull together a few materials which I think you'll find interesting for our company."*

2. **Presentation of accomplishments:** This section summarizes your major accomplishments. Focus on your top three to five accomplishments. As you do this, be sure to quantify your work by incorporating statistics about your achievements (*"expanded client base by four percent this past quarter"*). Also, give examples of what you did and explain how your work benefited the company.

3. **Changes in current position and job:** Remind your boss about the job you were hired to do. Note any changes that have taken place that are evidence of job growth and expansion. If your job has grown far beyond its original intent, explain what job you view you are really doing at present. If you believe what you are doing now is more accurately reflected in a new job or position title, mention what you believe your position really should be called given your new duties and responsibilities.

4. **Research on comparable positions:** Share with your boss some of your more interesting findings about comparable positions in other organizations, including duties and responsibilities (if they are equal or less than what you do), salaries, benefits, and perks (if they are more than what you currently receive), and any interesting incentivized pay schemes that might relate to your work. Note where you believe you stand in comparison to both the norm and to an equally comparable position in a similar type of organization.

5. **Current compensation package:** Refresh your boss's memory concerning the total value of your current compensation package. If you didn't get much of a raise last year, remind her of this situation as well as any previous discussions and commitments made for this year. Talk about your base salary but don't be preoccupied with this figure. Be sure to touch on several elements in your compensation package as well as any that may be absent, such as incentivized pay in the form of bonuses or stock options.

6. **Goals for next year:** Share with your boss some of your ideas for setting measurable goals for this coming year. These should be goals that can be quantified and thus clearly related to various compensation elements. For example, you plan to bring in $1 million in additional business which is $200,000 above what you did this year. Make sure you engage your boss in a discussion of measurable goals. You should establish these together. This critical stage in your presentation provides a powerful transition into the next item on your agenda, your proposed compensation package for this coming year.

7. **Proposed compensation package:** This is where redundancy is important. Your proposed compensation should be a function of (1) your current documented accomplishments, (2) your research findings on comparable positions and salaries, and (3) your measurable goals for this year. Consequently, summarize all three of these points again as a preface to detailing your proposed compensation package. Use some form of our "possibility question" when making your proposal. For example,

> *"Is it possible to work out a 10 to 25 percent increase in compensation for next year? This would involve a 10 percent increase in my base salary, which brings me in line with others in comparable positions. This increase also reflects an incentive provision that would give me a five percent bonus for each $100,000 in additional business I generate above my current annual sales of $800,000. This would cap at 15*

percent once I reached $300,000 in additional business. I would also expect an incentive bonus for anything in excess of $1.1 million in total business I generate for the year."

While such a request may initially appear excessive from the perspective of an employer who is used to giving 3-5 percent annual salary increments, it's quite reasonable considering what has been both presented (salary comparables) and proposed (a no risk, high return incentive plan). There's lots of room here for negotiation rather than outright rejection. As in this example, you may want to put special emphasis on incentivizing elements within your current compensation package rather than only focus on base salary. Be sure you set achievable targets rather than just expand the scope of your work for the sake of negotiating new compensation possibilities. If you pile too much on yourself, you may appear unrealistic and your performance may look like it has actually gone down when you next come up for a salary review.

8. **Summary and close:** Hopefully you've made an impressive presentation that motivates your boss to accept your proposal or at least to negotiate in the direction of the elements that defined your agenda. Depending on how your boss responds to your proposal, you should bring this meeting to a close by first summarizing your main points and then asking your boss when you can meet again after she has had a chance to consider your request. Hopefully another meeting will be scheduled shortly and a decision forthcoming within a few days, depending on the decision-making authority

of your boss. Your closing should result in some form
of closure, such as penciling in another meeting date, so
you both know what the next step will be in this salary
negotiation process.

Organize a Powerful One-Page Talking Paper

One of the best ways to focus your presentation and discussion is
to develop a one-page talking paper that you share with your boss.
Remember, this is not a wish list of things you would like to get
from the boss. Instead, it represents several issues you would like
to discuss concerning the structure of your job and compensation.

Representing a version of your agenda, this one-page talking
paper consists of "talking points" that should be rich in numbers
that quantify your performance, spec-
ify initiatives, and summarize alternative compensation elements. It should
be very performance oriented—indicates to the boss what you are accomplishing for the organization. Divide
this talking paper into two sections
and three columns—six panels altogether. The first column should summarize your current work and compensation situation. The second col-

> Your talking paper should be very performance oriented—indicates to the boss what you are accomplishing for the organization.

umn should include highlights from your research on comparable
positions and compensation. The third column should represent
proposed changes to your job and compensation. Keep the points
brief and simple. They should consist of keywords or phrases that
trigger important points you want to discuss with your boss. Your
one-page talking paper might look something like this:

Stacey Wynford
Marketing Manager, 1996-1998

Current	Comparables/Issues	Proposed Changes

Job Issues/Changes

Current	Comparables/Issues	Proposed Changes
■ Marketing Manager	■ Director of Marketing	■ Director of Marketing
■ key accomplishments	■ highlights	■ new targets
■ maintain key clients	■ client development	■ client development
■ develop budget	■ set spending targets	■ set spending targets
■ strategic marketing	■ PR/advertising efforts	■ PR/advertising efforts
■ special projects	■ new initiatives	■ new initiatives
■ telemarketing	■ database management	■ develop new database
■ monthly reports	■ weekly summaries	■ weekly summaries
■ quarterly briefings	■ biweekly newsletter	■ biweekly newsletter
■ traditional marketing	■ Internet marketing	■ Internet marketing
■ work station	■ office	■ office
■ office equipment	■ computer/cell phone	■ computer/cell phone

Compensation Issues/Changes

Current	Comparables/Issues	Proposed Changes
■ $35,000 base pay	■ $35-40,000 base pay	■ $38,000 base pay
■ no commissions	■ commissions/incentives	■ incentivized pay
■ 401 (k) plan (0% employer contribution)	■ 30% employer contribution	■ 30% employer contribution
■ yearly bonus	■ bonus + profit sharing	■ bonus + profit sharing
■ no company equity	■ stock options	■ stock options
■ 12 vacation days	■ 15-18 vacation days	■ 16 vacation days
■ no personal leave days	■ 3-5 personal leave days	■ 3 personal leave days
■ life insurance only	■ disability insurance	■ disability insurance
■ no child care	■ on-site child care	■ backup child care
■ training courses	■ tuition reimbursement	■ tuition reimbursement
■ consumer club	■ consumer + health club	■ consumer + health club

In Stacey's case, she focused her presentation and discussion on how her job functions had changed in relation to her original job description as well as in reference to comparable positions in other organizations. The point she wanted to stress was how much her job as Marketing Manager had grown beyond its original intent; it best approximated that of a Director of Marketing in several other companies she surveyed. Therefore, she felt she should be given a new job title that more accurately reflected her growing job functions. This is a good issue to start with because it has no immediate implications on compensation. The boss can easily accept such a proposal because it is backed by evidence (quantifiable) and not necessarily have implications for compensation (not as of yet!). She will probably have little difficulty giving Stacey this symbolic promotion by changing her job title from Marketing Manager to Director of Marketing. While it probably has greater meaning to Stacey than to the boss, it's probably a good morale booster that will motivate Stacey to better perform her "new" job.

The other elements in Stacey's talking paper stress her initiatives, from summarizing her accomplishments to noting how the position could be improved in reference to similar positions in other organizations as well as according to her own experience and insights. The compensation section then translates her expanded job functions into a new compensation package that moves her to an occupational norm as well as incentivizes her pay. The many talking points under compensation give Stacey and her boss a great deal of room to negotiate individual elements of this compensation package. In the end, Stacey may be talking about a 15 to 25 percent increase in her total compensation.

Use the following form to develop your own one-page talking paper. Be sure that your talking points emphasize the language of your boss—performance. Each element should be justified in terms of how it will benefit both you and the employer.

_____

_____

Current	Comparables/Issues	Proposed Changes

Job Issues/Changes

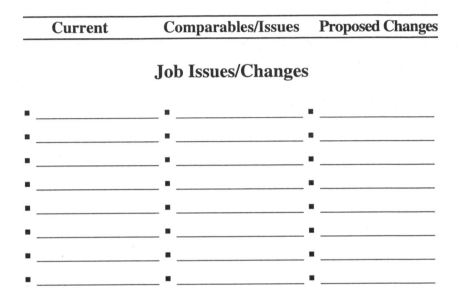

Compensation Issues/Changes

Overcome Nervousness

For many people, talking money to power is a high anxiety activity. They get anxious and nervous talking about a subject that is so ego involved and fraught with making mistakes, saying the wrong thing, or experiencing rejection. They often don't know what to say or they are afraid of saying the wrong thing; talking money to power does not come natural to them! Many people are naturally shy talking about their performance and monetary requirements. Similar to many people who grew up in the Midwest, they long ago learned not to talk about themselves or money; they were brought up to believe that only self-centered, arrogant, and obnoxious people would do such things. Indeed, this is the one meeting they would rather avoid.

If you feel you will be very nervous at this meeting, here are some things you can and should do to lessen your anxiety and put your best foot forward:

1. **Thoroughly prepare for the meeting** by planning the major points you will make and your supports for them. The hardest part will probably be to get started, so especially plan a good introduction that should immediately establish excellent rapport with your boss whose positive response should put you at ease.

2. **Keep focused on your message** rather than on yourself or your surroundings. It's the message that's most important in this meeting. Since you are well prepared, you should have a great deal to talk about.

3. **Make notes and practice mentally** what you will say to your boss during each phase of your presentation.

4. **Practice out loud what you plan to say.** Literally take yourself through your 20-minute presentation with your spouse or a friend. If you are alone, talk to a clock—it has a face and moves, and it gives you an opportunity to time your presentation! Tape-record or video-tape yourself and then listen or view the tape. Talking through your message gives you the opportunity to smooth out any rough spots and add supports (examples, statistics, etc.) if needed. It should help you feel better prepared for the meeting with your boss. However, *do not* try to memorize what you will say. At best, you will sound stilted and as if you have tried to memorize a speech. The worst case scenario is that, with the give-and-take of comments (interruptions) from your boss, you forget and draw a blank at some point. Your preparation should include planning the points you wish to make and determining your supporting data. But each time you go through a practice session, say the ideas with the words that come naturally to you at that point in time. This way your conversation with your boss will be what it should be: planned, but natural and spontaneous. Check your notes to make sure you follow your agenda, but don't worry about the exact words you use.

5. **Control your nervousness.** If you still feel nervous as you start you introduction, take a deep breath (from the diaphragm) and slow down (the tendency is to speed up a presentation or conversation when you're nervous).

6. **Watch your body language.** Since the greatest proportion of your message will be communicated non-verbally, be aware of your body language. Sit up

straight in your chair, with a slight forward lean into the conversation. Try to have a pleasant, interested and appropriately animated expression on your face. Make eye contact with your boss as you speak as well as listen. Try not to fidget or engage in other distracting behaviors.

Present Your Talking Paper

The best time to present your talking paper is at the very beginning of your meeting following any small talk. Do not give this paper to your boss prior to the meeting since doing so may confuse the is- sues and result in her taking control of your agenda. After you engage in the introductory small talk and then transition to the purpose of the meet- ing, ask if the two of you could look

Do not give your talking paper to your boss prior to the meeting.

at this paper for a few moments. You both should have your own copies. As you give her a copy, say something to this effect:

"I've put together some information on my position that I would like to discuss with you. Could we spend a few minutes going over some of these points?"

In fact, presentation of this talking paper will take more than just a few minutes. Chances are your talking paper will dominate 80 percent of the meeting, taking anywhere from one-half to one hour to discuss.

If your boss has scheduled this meeting and has a set agenda, you still want to bring your talking paper to this meeting. The best time to introduce this paper is when the boss's agenda turns to a discussion of your performance. As you talk about your accomplishments, try to transition to your talking paper.

In the end, you should be able to focus the agenda around your major talking points. Again, as we noted earlier, he who controls the agenda largely controls the outcomes of the meeting. Make sure you're at least in partial control and focused on what's really important to both you and your boss!

11

Develop a 3-Minute "Perfect Salary Pitch"

S cheduling the meeting and structuring the setting puts you at the right place at the right time. These actions also put you "on track"—focus on exactly what you want to communicate to your boss and hope to gain in new compensation. However, you also need to stay on message. One of the ways to do this is to develop a 3-minute "Perfect Salary Pitch."

Pitching Your Value

While the meeting with your boss may last 30 to 60 minutes, you need to be able to pitch your case in as succinct a manner as possible. You do this through what we call the powerful 3-minute "Perfect Salary Pitch." In the space of three minutes, you need to answer your bosses' key questions which she may or may not ask you directly:

"Why should I give you a raise? What will it cost me?"

Let's assume raises are not given automatically by your boss. Instead, raises reflect two important considerations:

1. The rate of inflation or cost of living

2. Your special performance

In other words, one part of a raise may be automatic (inflation induced) depending on economic circumstances, while the other part needs to be earned. It's this second part—your perfor-mance—that needs to be measured and communicated to your boss. A raise based on performance is usually given when performance *exceeds* what is normally expected for a posi-tion.

> **Raises based on perfor-mance are *earned.* They *exceed* expectations for the position.**

For example, let's assume the rate of inflation is less than 1 percent. Therefore, your cost of living has not significantly increased unless you made some important lifestyle changes that have inflated your cost of living. But lifestyle changes are choices *you* make rather than larger economic forces that are beyond your immediate control. Your employer may feel responsible for giving you a cost of living salary increase, but chances are she has no interest in contributing to your new lifestyle choices. If the rate of inflation is very low, don't expect an automatic cost of living increase to be included in your raise. You'll have to convince her that your performance has been extraordinary for the year. This is where your 3-minute "Perfect Salary Pitch" comes in.

Pitching your value to your employer will be the most important thing you can do to affect your raise. But it's more than just value.

After all, you are being employed because of your value. It's your *added value* that needs to be communicated for a raise. And it's your "Perfect Salary Pitch" that will emphasize your added value. Whatever you do, don't recite in your "Perfect Salary Pitch" a level of performance that is already expected for your position. If you do this, your pitch will be more than just "off track." It may say that you would like to be paid more for doing what you're already expected to do. This is not an added-value approach.

As you prepare your "Perfect Salary Pitch," begin thinking about what you did to add value to your position. List those things that you are expected to do versus those things that you have done to add new value to the position.

Your Performance Record

Expected	Added-Value

When you develop your "Perfect Salary Pitch," focus on those things that you have done to add new value to both the position and the organization. For when you add value and communicate it loud and clear to your boss, you also set the stage for adding greater compensation for your superior performance.

Language That Speaks On Target

There's nothing really complicated about developing a powerful salary "pitch." Make it very simple, targeted, and functionally redundant. Your language should emphasize goals, actions, results, and outcomes. *Quantify* as much as possible what you did and give *examples* of how your actions benefited the organization. Avoid reciting formal duties and responsibilities or describing your workload. Instead of saying,

> **Your "pitch" should be very simple, targeted, and functionally redundant.**

"I completed 25 biweekly reports on time."

On time performance should be expected of every employee. Remember, you need to *exceed* the expectations for the job and use language that focuses on results. Therefore, restate this expected work activity in the action language identified with specific results, outcomes, and benefits:

> *"Five of my 25 biweekly reports resulted in redesigning the marketing department which, in turn, generated 20 percent in additional business over a six month period. Several recommendations appearing in the other reports will soon be implemented."*

In other words, when deciding how to talk about your work, think in terms of (1) what was the outcome of my work, (2) which outcomes exceeded the basic performance level for the job, and (3) who really benefited and with what results? If you can't talk about your work in these terms, you may want to reconsider talking about your work at all. Again, you are not building a case for greater compensation for just doing your assigned work. Your work must go beyond the basic duties of the job and be related to results and outcomes. It should demonstrate that you take initiative and are indispensable to the organization.

Key Elements Defining a Powerful "Pitch"

To be most effective, your 3-minute "Perfect Salary Pitch" should incorporate several important elements presented in the following sequence:

1. **A transition statement relating to previous discussions of your salary:** This initial statement provides an important linkage to what you discussed earlier, any previous agreements you made, and specific goals you had set. If, for example, you had a salary review last year, start the meeting with a statement such as this:

    "As we discussed in last year's meeting, we would re-address the question of incentivizing various aspects of my compensation package when I exceeded our agreed upon target of $60,000 in seminar sells each month. In fact, during the past four months I've been able to exceed our targets by at least $20,000 a month. My new telemarketing system is now in place and seems to be working

very well. Best of all, I think I'll be able to top $100,000 a month beginning next month. I've put in a lot of special effort to make this possible."

This is a very powerful transition statement that sets the stage for negotiating higher compensation. It immediately reminds the boss of your agreement last year about re-addressing the compensation question. Encompassing the past, present, and future, as well as quantifying performance, it quickly incorporates three additional elements that will remain constant themes throughout your 3-minute "Perfect Salary Pitch":

➤ **Expected performance**—as defined by specific targeted goals you and your boss agreed upon.

➤ **Added-value performance**—that which goes beyond the expected and thus sets the stage improving your compensation package.

➤ **Projected future performance**—extends your current added-value performance into the future with quantifiable targets; provides additional rationale for improving your compensation package.

2. **Summary of your top three accomplishments which are expected for your position:** This element reaffirms the fact that you are doing your job as expected. Indeed, you are fully earning your current level of compensation. If you feel your boss may have some questions about what you have actually accomplished during the

year, or if you have failed to clearly communicate your accomplishments during the year, here's the opportunity to lay out your contributions in a very succinct and quantifiable manner. For example, you might say:

"During this past year we were really successful in accomplishing three major goals we established last August: (1) increased our technical training programs by 12 percent in the overseas market; (2) developed our new training-on-demand Web site which generated over $100,000 in electronic commerce during the first six months; and (3) improved the profitability of our on-site government training contracts by 15 percent."

Then briefly embellish each accomplishment in terms of what you did and how it benefited the company.

3. **Examples of three added-value accomplishments:** This is the most important element since it focuses on what new accomplishments should be rewarded with greater compensation. Here you outline those things that go beyond the expected and for which you have not really been compensated—at least not yet. For example, you may say:

"The really good news is that I also was able to (1) develop new Web-based training relationships with two major marketing firms which will be offering our online products to their current military clients; (2) expand our overseas markets into both Australia and Singapore; and (3) increase our market share of CD-ROM supervisory training products by four

*percent which represented a 20 percent increase in
overall sales for last year."*

4. **Outline three new performance targets for the year:**
    These are "promises" that reinforce your added-value
    accomplishments. Here you communicate to your boss
    that you have a plan for improved performance in the
    coming year. Focus here on both the bottomline and
    innovative ideas, performance targets that should be
    enthusiastically embraced by your boss who sees you as
    someone who is a self-starter and takes initiative that's
    in perfect alignment with the goals of the organization.
    For example, you might say:

    > *"I'm really excited about pushing forward during
    > the next few months with (1) a new electronic
    > commerce strategy that will more than double our
    > online training revenue; (2) an expanded overseas
    > market which will include the rapidly expanding
    > high-tech centers in southern and central India; and
    > (3) further expanding the market share of our new
    > financial planning CD-ROM programs. I think
    > we're on the verge of some major breakthroughs in
    > markets that only two years ago looked extremely
    > risky. I'm really looking forward to expanding the
    > areas in which we laid important ground work
    > during this last year. Do you agree we should be
    > concentrating our next efforts here?"*

5. **Repetition of the first four elements should continue
    throughout the meeting in the form of a 30-word
    added-value phrase:** Redundancy is a virtue during
    this meeting, especially when it re-emphasizes your

value to the employer. You might condense the first four elements into a statement like this:

"I've contributed greatly to expanding our client base, market shares, and profitability. I plan to continue doing so as well as develop innovative strategies to further grow our business."

If, for example, your boss asks you what you are expecting for a raise (*'What are you expecting this year?"*) or if she tells what it will likely be (*"We've decided to give you an 8 percent raise."*), incorporate your 30-word "added-value phrase" in your response:

"Is a 15 to 20% increase possible? Let me explain why I think this would be fair. I've found this is in line with what others in similar positions of other organizations, who have comparable responsibilities, are making. Most important of all, it reflects the fact that I've contributed greatly to expanding our client base, market shares, and profitability. I plan to continue doing so as well

> **Redundancy is virtual in this situation. Be creative in restating the same ideas that focus on your value to the employer.**

as develop innovative strategies to further grow our business. My performance for this coming year should more than justify this increase. An 8 percent increase would not really bring me up to what others make in this position, much less reflect my extra effort in bringing in new business. Any thoughts about incentivizing my compensation?"

Try to constantly interject this "added-value phrase" throughout your meeting, but try to think of alternative ways of saying the same thing. Remember, this 30-word statement is the single most important message you want your boss to hear over and over and over. But you should not sound like a broken record by saying the same words over and over and over again. Be creative in restating the same ideas that focus on your value to the employer. You can easily do this by moving to different levels of observation and abstraction, from specific examples to a synthesis of results. For example, if you restate your "Perfect Salary Pitch" at the level of concrete examples, you might say:

> **Be creative in restating the same message in different words.**

"Is a 15 to 20% increase possible? Let me explain why I think this would be fair. I've found this is in line with what others in similar positions of other organizations, who have comparable responsibilities, are making. Most important of all, it reflects the fact that <u>I've improved the profitability of our department by 20%; expanded our e-commerce 100%; and we are well on our way to generating $700,000 in revenue from our new Indian operations.</u> My performance for this coming year should more than justify this increase. An 8 percent increase would not really bring me up to what others make in this position, much less reflect my extra effort in bringing in new business. Any thoughts about incentivizing my compensation?"

Keep On Message

Keep repeating some form of your 30-word "added-value phrase" at different times and within different contexts during the meeting with your boss. Under no circumstances should you memorize these statements. If you do, chances are they will sound contrived and insincere. Worst of all, you will probably be nervous throughout your meeting because of your fear of forgetting your "lines." Know the general points you want to make and terminology you need to use and keep focused on your very simple message—your added-value for the employer's added compensation. Your mission is very simple and what you want seems quite fair and reasonable—to share in the very wealth that you helped generate for your employer. You need to be compensated commensurate to your performance so you can continue generating additional wealth for your employer.

12

Anticipate Objections to Your Pitch

Regardless of how well you prepare for your meeting, structure the situation, or develop a 3-minute "Perfect Salary Pitch," you will most likely encounter objections to your new compensation requirements. These objections come in many forms and require anticipation and special preparation to develop thoughtful responses that continue to keep you on message.

Types of Objections

It would be great if your boss responded to your presentation by saying, *"Yes, you're doing a great job. We'll be happy to give you what you're asking!"* A more likely response will be, *"That's out of the question. We're prepared to do the following . . ."* or *"Yes, I understand where you're coming from, but we're not going to be able to because . . . ."* Your boss will most likely go on to give you one of five standard objections presented to employees for not giving them the raise they want:

- It's not in our budget.
- It's more than others make here.
- Can't justify it to my boss.
- You're becoming too expense.
- This isn't a good time—maybe next year.

You need to prepare responses to each of these objections as well as to any others your boss might advance at this critical stage of your salary meeting.

Types of Responses

This is not the time to be clever nor to personalize your response to any objections relating to your presentation. While you may take an objection personally—interpreting it as a rejection of your worth—you must avoid doing so. Remember, you are now at a critical stage in your salary negotiations— the period immediately following your presentation—where you must stay on message: your exceptional performance for the employer's additional compensation. If there has ever been a time when you want to be redundant, it definitely is now! Under no circumstances should you fall back on weak, self-centered, and dumb responses, such as *"Well, it didn't hurt to try," "I really need a raise this year given my additional expenses,"* or *"How would you like to live on my salary?"* These are totally inappropriate comments given the situation and your previous focused presentation. To

> **This is not the time to be clever nor to personalize responses to objections.**

respond in any of these manners would invalidate the very points you made in your powerful presentation.

Armed with your 3-minute "Perfect Salary Pitch," you should be able to handle each of the five objections with ease. Regardless of whatever objections your boss advances, you must respond in a very thoughtful yet assertive manner. If you just sit there and act compliant by saying *"Okay, thanks for your time,"* the outcomes will be predictable: the meeting will be over, the employer will win, and you will have wasted at least seven days of preparation time. Your goal should be to walk away from this meeting with a better compensation package than you started with, one that is better than the one your employer was initially prepared to offer. In other words, you will most likely need to negotiate your continuing terms of employment around both your talking points and your boss's objections to your new compensation requirements.

It's Not in Our Budget

This is the standard feel-our-pain argument for limiting raises—*"it's not in the budget."* This objection comes in several forms:

- The company is not doing well this year.
- We're having to cutback our operations.
- The economy is in bad shape.
- We're having to hire new personnel.
- The expansion of our operations has meant belt tightening for everyone.
- I'm not even going to get a raise this year.
- I wish I could be more optimistic and forthcoming, but things have not been looking good for the company these past two quarters.

- I would have to layoff someone to meet your new salary requirements.

Let's assume these are legitimate concerns, and you're being asked to share the pain. After all, the company is not in great financial shape and employee compensation may constitute 60 percent of your company's expenses. When the bean counters come around to cut costs, there are no sacred cows other than the company's pension system. They often look at employee compensation as eating away at the bottomline. Generous pay packages established during the recent years of a booming economy may need to be re-examined in light of the company's new financial realities. Consequently, the cost cutters may want to adjust everyone's compensation downward or at least put it on hold for now—few if any raises to be given this year. In fact, your boss may need to talk to you about "givebacks"—actually lowering your salary and benefits and eliminating some of your perks!

So what are you going to do when presented with such a situation? Let's take the worst case scenario since responding to it reveals some important negotiating principles you might incorporate in other types of responses. Your boss responds to your presentation by saying this:

"You're not going to like what I'm about to say. Given our difficult financial situation, we have to cut salaries by 10 percent this year. Everyone is affected, including myself. We'll try to make it up to you next year, assuming we bounce back from what we see as some temporary setbacks. We certainly don't want to lose you since, as you've just indicated, you're a very valuable member of our team. But the bottomline is that we simply don't have the money to even meet our current payroll. We're asking you to help us through this difficult period."

Other than being laid off, it doesn't get much tougher than this. In fact, you may be shocked to discover you are apparently dealing in a non-negotiable situation. You may be lucky to keep your job, much less your current pay level!

Is there anything you can negotiate when your boss has just informed you that company policy is to take away employee compensation in exchange for a vague verbal "promise" of increased compensation sometime in the future? This is the perfect time to hammer out a new compensation agreement that will guarantee you greater compensation for increased performance. Begin thinking about a new win-win relationship between you and the employer. You want to present your boss with some low-risk but high-return alternatives affecting your future compensation. The best approach is to focus on incentivizing your pay package—your pay will be adjusted in direct response to your added contributions to the company's

> **If faced with a cutback situation, think about developing a new win-win relationship with your employer.**

profitability. As discussed earlier, you do this by developing *indicators* for the work you do and then relating them to specific payoffs, such as bonuses or company equity in the form of stock or stock options. If, for example, you generate $500,000 in additional business for the firm, you should receive a 1 or 2 percent bonus or 1000 shares of company stock. If you save the company $50,000, you should receive another 1 or 2 percent bonus or 10 shares of company stock. But let's say you're in a position that does not lend itself well to standard sales performance indicators. For example, you're a paralegal who essentially does a lot of research and writing. In this case, begin tieing your work to special contributions you've made to cases. How much value did any special work, for example, add to particular cases? What is this value worth in terms of a special bonus?

By incentivizing your compensation, you focus on what's really important to the employer—bottomline performance—and you establish indicators that can be easily converted into targets that motivate you to do an even better job. This is the classic win-win model—your increased performance in exchange for the employer's increased profitability. Everyone wins here, especially the employer who really needs increased performance from employees and who is reluctant to continue increasing base pay which will further inflate personnel costs. The major risk here is to your reputation—can you do what you say you'll probably do? If you can negotiate incentivized pay provisions in this situation, you may actually come out ahead in what was ostensibly a cutback situation where most employees agree to downsize their base pay and give up some benefits and perks. You, on the other hand, were smart enough to set up a scheme that enabled you to actually increase your compensation. Best of all, you're getting this in writing so it will become a permanent element in your compensation package. Your boss's verbal promise of "making it up" to employees at a later date will probably become eroded in time. You may want to get your compensation promises in writing.

Once you've negotiated this worst case scenario, all the other objections concerning *"it's not in the budget"* can be easily dealt with from a similar perspective. Your best approach will be to stay on message with a proposal to:

1. maintain your current base pay, benefits, and perks

2. incentivize your added-value performance (Chapter 11)

Focusing on rewarding added-value performance in the form of a bonus or equity in the company makes good sense to most employers who really understand their most important resource is a highly talented and motivated workforce. If, on the other hand, your employer has not thought about incentivized pay, you may need to educate him on how such schemes work in other companies and especially how they can potentially benefit everyone.

It's More Than Others Make Here

Let's face it. Most employers want to be on the cutting edge of new products and services, but they really don't want to be on the cutting edge of employee compensation packages. They prefer following the leader rather than being the leader when it comes to employee pay. If your new compensation requirements appear to be at the cutting edge for your position, expect this classic red flag to begin waving as your employer wants to avoid being a pay pacesetter: *"It's more than others make here."*

> **Few employers want to be on the cutting edge of employee compensation packages. They would rather follow the leader.**

However, this may be the easiest objection to deal with. You are less concerned about comparing your compensation to others in your organization than being compared to others in comparable organizations. In other words, you want to be compared externally rather than internally. While your employer tends to view each employee's compensation relative to other employees in the organization, you've done your research on salary comparables in other organizations. Therefore, you should know your market value. Your response to this objection might be this:

> *"I really don't know what others make here nor would I think others know what I make here. I've never really been concerned about co-workers' salaries since I don't think it's any of my business. However, I do know what Directors of*

Marketing with similar responsibilities make in comparable organizations. According to the most recent study of the American Marketing Association, the average compensation package of Directors of Marketing in office supply companies with 500 to 1000 employees is valued at $87,342. I've figured my compensation package to be worth $76,500. Is there some reason why Office Star is nearly 15 percent behind the industry norm?"

By shifting from an internal to an external comparison, you force your boss to look at compensation from a much larger perspective. You, in effect, let him know that your company may not be competitive in today's job market. Recruiting and retaining talent is potentially a problem because of compensation differentials. This should be of great concern to any employer who wants to remain competitive in today's talent-driven economy. Indeed, your little comparative compensation revelation may come as a surprise to your boss who now needs to rethink his compensation strategy. Hopefully, he'll move closer to your numbers because he feels he must be competitive in today's market.

Can't Justify It to My Boss

This is a rather lame excuse for not being effective with one's boss. Again, keep on message. Repeat your 3-minute "Perfect Salary Pitch" in a form that enables your boss to communicate it directly to his boss. Your boss needs to emphasize to management how important you are to the organization. Give him a good rationale, as well as statistics and examples, from which he can present your case to his boss. Keep in mind that management also wants to attract and retain talented employees who can contribute to the bottomline. And management will probably present the same objections to your boss as he presents to you. Consider your reasoned "on message" responses to be a dress rehearsal for your boss who also must talk money to power.

You're Becoming Too Expensive

You may elicit another classic objection if your boss feels he's in the driver's seat—*"You're becoming too expensive."* This is another variation of the *"It's more than others make here"* objection. And it's another comparative statement—too expensive in comparison to whom or what? Chances are the comparison is with other employees or in relation to the overall costs of personnel. If you repeat your "Perfect Salary Pitch," you will re-emphasize your added-value to the organization. You should not be viewed as a simple accounting expense. Instead, you are an opportunity cost. You might respond by saying something like this:

> *"I've never really considered myself as a company expense. I feel I've really been contributing to the company, especially during these past six months when we were able to sign on three big accounts. What I'm requesting is that my compensation be adjusted in relationship to my increased value. I want to see this company grow; I want to be a major part of the growth; and I want to be fairly compensated for my contribution to that growth. Isn't this what Office Star wants, too?"*

This Isn't a Good Time—Maybe Next Year

If your boss tries to avoid your request by postponing it until some later date, don't let this opportunity pass by agreeing to wait until some future date. After all, you've presented a very strong case, perhaps stronger than it will be next year. You've outlined options. You're willing to negotiate. Most important of all, your time is now. To put you off until next year is really unfair. Smart employers know such shortsighted actions can be detrimental to your morale and thus dysfunctional to the organization. If this objection is advanced, you might respond in this manner:

> *"I really need to make some decisions about my future with this company. Could we take another look at my proposal, especially the incentivized pay provisions which should tremendously benefit the company? If we wait until next year, we may lose some real opportunities in the meantime."*

Your opening line will get your boss's attention—you could be thinking of leaving and thus ratcheting up the company's recruitment and training costs! The other lines should persuade him to take another look at this issue. Perhaps this could be a real win-win situation. Assuming this may not be a good time to talk about money, because of the company's questionable financial situation, it's best to deal with the compensation issue in the same manner you dealt with the first objection—*"It's not in the budget."* Focus on incentivizing your pay package. If you do this, your boss may discover this is a very good time to deal with the issue! You both could walk away with the ultimate package—no risk, high return.

When Objections Cannot Be Overcome

Sometimes employers simply don't want to negotiate with employees nor do they want to listen to proposals that wander outside their compensation blinders; changing the way they determine compensation (top-down) may be threatening to their whole system of labor-management relations. If the answer is "no" and there is no apparent room for negotiation and compromise, all is not lost. You should read this response as a sign that it is now time to re-evaluate your relationship with your employer. Indeed, you should be sensing that this may not be the type of organization you want to continue investing more time and effort with since it is not competitive in the marketplace nor very responsive to the concerns of its employees.

As we noted earlier, how you negotiate your salary with your employer will affect your relationship with the employer. The flip-side of this principle is this: how willing your employer is to deal with your compensation concerns should be a good indicator of how well your relationship will evolve in the future. It may be time to consider new employment options which could substantially improve your total compensation package. At least this exercise in talking money to power will have identified key issues and outlined a sound strategy for talking money to future employers. You will have created a very strong database on both yourself and your occupation for deciding whether it is time to find a more compensation-friendly employer who may more fully appreciate your value in today's job market.

Times Do Change

Several of the previous scenarios, of course, are predicated upon the research you did earlier on salary comparables. Make certain the comparisons you are making are valid:

- that you are comparing your position to *very* similar positions—not just by title but also by responsibilities and functions

- that the economy in general and your industry in particular have not been negatively affected between the time the salary surveys you consulted were conducted and the time you are meeting with your boss.

For if major downward changes take place within the economy to depress your industry, you could leave your current employer only to find what you had was pretty good after all!

13

Close and Follow-Up With Impact

I t's not over until you reach agreement and walk away with a new compensation package that is satisfactory to both you and your boss. At this stage you need to reach closure as well as reaffirm your continuing professional relationship with your boss. How you handle the close and follow-up stage will be important to maintaining a quality relationship.

Summarize Your Understanding

After you've presented your "Perfect Salary Pitch" and handled any objections to your proposal, it's time to bring closure to this meeting. One of the best ways to do this is to summarize the jist of the meeting. This summary pulls together the major issues raised in the meeting, confirms your understanding of the boss's position, and focuses on taking action centered around your proposal. Being redundant once again, your summary should incorporate several of the same points you made in your "Perfect Salary Pitch." Your summary might go like this:

"If I understand correctly, you feel I should receive a 5 percent increase in base pay which really reflects a cost-of-living increase plus an across-the-board increase. Since this increase is not really related to my performance, you would prefer to reward performance with an annual bonus. However, I'm unclear how this bonus will be figured since you still need to speak with your boss about my proposed plan for incentive pay based on performance. I'm also concerned about a few other issues, such as disability insurance and contributions to my 401 (k) plan. As I mentioned earlier, I believe my work this past year has been exceptional, especially considering the $400,000 in additional business I brought to the company. With two new big accounts coming on board within the next month, I'm very concerned that my efforts be better compensated. If you recall, my compensation package still lags about 15 percent behind many others I know in this business. When do you think you'll be able to get back with me about my proposal? Would it be possible to talk sometime next week?"

This summary refocuses the discussion around the main compensation issues as well as emphasizes the importance of bringing closure to the compensation issues you raised. It requests that action to be taken soon.

If It's a "Go"

If you are so fortunate to find your boss in complete agreement with your compensation proposal, close the meeting with a big "thank you" and a reaffirmation of your commitment to the organization and your boss. Say something like this:

> *"I really appreciate your support. As you know, Office Star is a very special place for me. I've learned a great deal about marketing, and I work with some of the best people in the business. What I really appreciate is your willingness to deal with these important compensation issues. I'm pleased we're able to work out a new compensation plan that should further motivate me to become one of your top performers."*

This is simply a nice thing to say to your boss. It reaffirms your positive relationship with your boss and your loyalty to the company. Before you leave this meeting, ask about getting the agreement in writing and clarify when you might expect to see your salary increase reflected in your paycheck:

> *"Will you be putting this agreement in writing? I would appreciate a letter or memo that summarizes our agreement. Also, when will the 5 percent salary increase begin appearing in my paycheck?"*

Try to get important compensation agreements in writing. Verbal commitments can result in misunderstandings, and your boss today may not be your boss tomorrow. If it's important to you, it should be in writing.

A final thing you should do is send your boss a typed thank you letter in which you reiterate in writing what you said to him in person. This is a very thoughtful thing to do, and employers like thoughtful employees. They remember them as good employees. You always want to be remembered as such because it means developing a good relationship with your boss. Best of all, bosses hate to say "no" to their favorite employees!

If It's a "Maybe"

If the conclusion of this meeting seems to be uncertain, restate your case in summary form, including another version of your "Perfect Salary Pitch," and then ask when a final decision might be made:

> *"I know you still need to give this some more thought as well as discuss it with management. When do you think you'll have an answer? Would you like me to prepare some additional materials for your meeting with management? For example, I have some comparative salary figures relating to my position."*

This response attempts to bring closure to the compensation issue. Better still, it offers supports to the boss who must move the compensation issue to another decision-making level. Helpful employees also are liked by their bosses. They are more likely to become your advocate because you helped them build your case.

If It's a "No"

If the response to your compensation request is "no," try to close the meeting by leaving the door open for continuing negotiations. You might do so as follows:

> *"While I'm disappointed in the raise I'm getting this year, I still have several compensation issues I would like to discuss with you. I would appreciate a more thorough performance review within the next three months. And I would also like to present you with a detailed proposal about some changes in my compensation package. Would it be okay if I sent you a*

proposal next week? It includes several ideas that I think you'll find interesting."

If your boss is resistant to such an initiative, it's probably time to begin reassessing your job, your skills, and your job search capabilities. This may be a good time to start "testing the waters" by putting together a resume, examining job sites on the Internet, and networking for information, advice, and referrals. The failure of your boss to deal with your compensation concerns is grounds for you to broaden your job horizons!

Effective Follow-Ups

Don't forget to follow-up your meeting, regardless of its outcome. The purpose of follow-up is to make things happen—get your boss to take action. If your boss agrees to your compensation requests, the most appropriate follow-up—one that will strengthen your relationship and affect next year's salary meeting—is the thank you letter. Sincerely express your appreciation, gratitude, and loyalty in this letter. These are qualities that make employees "likable" in the eyes of employers. They help cement professional relationships and promote personal relationships.

If your boss says "maybe" to your request, follow-up with more information on your performance. This might be in the form of statistics, testimonials, or proposals—anything that will influence the final decision and is related to your contributions to the organization.

If your boss says "no" to your request, follow-up with a thank you letter in which you thank your boss for his time and consideration. Express your disappointment in not receiving the raise you wanted, but stress how important you feel a three-month performance review would be to both you and the company. Ask to have such a meeting to review your performance. Such a letter may well turn what is an obvious negative into a long-term positive relationship. If you really enjoy your job and the people you work with, you can eventually overcome such rejections. It requires savvy follow-up work and persistence in making your case about rewarding your performance.

14

Then Do What You're Worth

It's one thing to talk about performance and another to deliver the goods. Throughout this book we've stressed the importance of focusing on your performance vis-a-vis the employer's needs. If you want to get a raise, you must be employer-centered rather than self-centered. What is it that makes you so exceptional? How does your employer really benefit from your work? What specific contributions have you made to the bottom line? Are you delivering results that can be quantified and rewarded accordingly?

If you can't answer these questions with examples, perhaps you shouldn't be talking about a raise at all. Just doing your job according to expectations is not enough to justify a raise in today's job world.

You Must Be Exceptional Rather Than Accepting

This final step is really the most important to getting a raise, keeping your job, and advancing in your career. This is the step that "delivers the goods"—you literally do what you say rather than just say what you think your employer wants to hear from you. You must do more than play roles, give superficial lip service to the latest employee-management jargon, and constantly engage in on-the-job PR. You're a person of real substance who is more concerned about doing a good job than looking good on the job.

Performance is the single most important element employers look for on resumes, probe for during job interviews, and focus on in performance evaluations and salary reviews. While they are interested in hearing about your achievements and listening to your catalog of who, what, where, and when stories, they are really looking for evidence that you have an exceptional *pattern of performance*. Do you do what you say and say what you do? Are you an exceptional employee who rises above the crowd? Are you worthy of additional compensation that is the mark of the exceptional employee or do you just do your job according to expectations?

> **You should be a person of real substance who is more concerned about doing a good job than looking good on the job.**

If you want to be most effective in getting a raise, you must impress your boss as being someone who is indispensable to the organization. If you're not considered today's indispensable person, chances are you may become tomorrow's disposable employee. You must communicate your performance qualities throughout the year rather than once a year in a performance evaluation or salary review meeting. Exceptional employees understand and focus on both substance and language. They demonstrate as well as communicate the key qualities employers look for when dispensing on-the-job rewards.

Document Your Results

If you are not doing so now, it's time that you begin documenting your performance on a regular basis so that you are in a better position to "tell your stories" to your boss. You must think and act like an entrepreneur—what can I do to make my company more profitable? Are there certain things I should be doing that would better contribute to the bottomline? We recommend keeping a weekly diary in which you summarize those things that you've accomplished for the week. Divide it in half and record

> **You must think and act like an entrepreneur—what can I do to make my company more profitable?**

what it is you did that is expected (good works) versus exceptional (exceptional works). It might look something like this:

My Good Works	My Exceptional Works

Getting a raise will most likely depend on the quality of information that appears in the second column ("My Exceptional Work"). These are your *stories of success* that should culminate in your *pattern of performance*.

Make a Habit of Your Success

Getting a raise in seven days is really not that difficult as long as you've been doing good work—cumulating successes throughout the year and communicating them to your boss. For in the end, you don't need to come up with clever negotiating strategies and techniques to convince your employer that you should get a raise. Assume your boss is smart enough to recognize exceptional work. He recognizes your

> **Raises should only be expected if they are earned.**

exceptional work because you've made a habit of success. To do only what is expected and then expect a raise is simply not how the work world operates these days.

Raises should only be expected if they are earned. They are *earned* by those who know how to talk money to power because they exude a pattern of performance that speaks loud and clear to their employer. If you follow our seven day plan for getting a raise and you do indeed get the raise you want, power will recognize you as an exceptional employee. If your seven day journey to salary success is less than satisfactory, start today in building your portfolio of successes that will become the basis for your powerful presentation in next year's salary review!

Index

The Authors

Ronald L. Krannich, Ph.D. and Caryl Rae Krannich, Ph.D.,
are two of America's leading business and travel writers who have
authored more than 40 books. They currently operate Development
Concepts Inc., a training, consulting, and publishing firm. A
former Peace Corps Volunteer and Fulbright Scholar, Ron
received his Ph.D. in Political Science from Northern Illinois
University. Caryl received her Ph.D. in Speech Communication
from Penn State University.

Ron and Caryl are former university professors, high school
teachers, management trainers, and consultants. As trainers and
consultants, they have completed numerous projects on management, career development, local government, population planning,
and rural development in the United States and abroad.

The Krannichs' business and career work encompasses nearly
30 books they have authored on a variety of subjects: key job
search skills, public speaking, government jobs, international
careers, nonprofit organizations, and career transitions. Their work
represents one of today's most extensive and highly praised

collections of career and business writing: *101 Dynamite Answers to Interview Questions, 101 Secrets of Highly Effective Speakers, 201 Dynamite Job Search Letters, The Best Jobs For the 21st Century, Change Your Job Change Your Life, The Complete Guide to International Jobs and Careers, Discover the Best Jobs For You, Dynamite Cover Letters, Dynamite Resumes, Dynamite Salary Negotiations, Dynamite Tele-Search, The Educator's Guide to Alternative Jobs and Careers, Find a Federal Job Fast, From Air Force Blue to Corporate Gray, From Army Green to Corporate Gray, From Navy Blue to Corporate Gray, Resumes and Job Search Letters For Transitioning Military Personnel, High Impact Resumes and Letters, International Jobs Directory, Interview For Success, Jobs and Careers With Nonprofit Organizations, Jobs For People Who Love Travel,* and *Dynamite Networking For Dynamite Jobs.* Their books are found in most major bookstores, libraries, and career centers. They also can be purchased through Impact's Web site: *www.impactpublications. com* and at the end of this book. Many of their works are available interactively on CD-ROM (*The Ultimate Job Source*).

Ron and Caryl live a double career life. Authors of 13 travel books, the Krannichs continue to pursue their international interests through their innovative and highly acclaimed Impact Guides travel series (*"The Treasures and Pleasures....Best of the Best"*) which currently encompasses separate titles on Italy, France, China, Hong Kong, Thailand, Indonesia, Singapore, Malaysia, India, and Australia. When not found at their home and business in Virginia, they are probably somewhere in Europe, Asia, Africa, the Middle East, the South Pacific, or the Caribbean pursuing one of their major passions—researching and writing about travel to quality arts and antiques.

The Krannichs reside in Northern Virginia. Frequent speakers and seminar leaders, they can be contacted through the publisher or by email: *krannich@impactpublications.com*

Career Resources

C ontact Impact Publications for a free annotated listing of career resources or visit their World Wide Web site for a complete listing of career resources: *www.impactpublications.com*.

The following career resources, many of which were mentioned in previous chapters, are available directly from Impact Publications. Complete the following form or list the titles, include postage (see formula at the end), enclose payment, and send your order to:

IMPACT PUBLICATIONS
9104-N Manassas Drive
Manassas Park, VA 20111-5211
1-800-361-1055 (orders only)
Tel. 703/361-7300 or Fax 703/335-9486
E-mail address: *raise@impactpublications.com*

Orders from individuals must be prepaid by check, moneyorder, Visa, MasterCard, or American Express. We accept telephone and fax orders.

Qty.	TITLES	Price	TOTAL
Job Search Strategies and Tactics			
___	Change Your Job, Change Your Life	17.95	___
___	Complete Idiot's Guide to Getting the Job You Want	24.95	___
___	Complete Job Finder's Guide to the 90's	13.95	___
___	Five Secrets to Finding a Job	12.95	___
___	How to Succeed Without a Career Path	13.95	___
___	Me, Myself, and I, Inc	17.95	___
___	New Rites of Passage at $100,000+	29.95	___
___	The Pathfinder	14.00	___

____ What Color Is Your Parachute?   16.95 _____
____ Who's Running Your Career   14.95 _____

Best Jobs and Employers For the 21st Century

____ 50 Coolest Jobs in Sports   15.95 _____
____ Adams Jobs Almanac 1998   15.95 _____
____ American Almanac of Jobs and Salaries   20.00 _____
____ Best Jobs For the 21st Century   19.95 _____
____ Breaking and Entering: Jobs in Film Production   17.95 _____
____ Great Jobs Ahead   11.95 _____
____ Jobs 1998   15.00 _____
____ The Top 100   19.95 _____

Key Directories

____ American Salaries and Wages Survey   110.00 _____
____ Business Phone Book USA 1999   160.00 _____
____ Careers Encyclopedia   39.95 _____
____ Complete Guide to Occupational Exploration   39.95 _____
____ Consultants & Consulting Organizations Directory   605.00 _____
____ Dictionary of Occupational Titles   47.95 _____
____ Encyclopedia of American Industries 1998   520.00 _____
____ Encyclopedia of Associations 1999 (all 3 volumes)   1260.00 _____
____ Encyclopedia of Associations 1998 (National only)   490.00 _____
____ Encyclopedia of Careers & Vocational Guidance   149.95 _____
____ Enhanced Guide For Occupational Exploration   34.95 _____
____ Enhanced Occupational Outlook Handbook   34.95 _____
____ Job Hunter's Sourcebook   70.00 _____
____ National Job Bank 1999   350.00 _____
____ National Trade & Professional Associations 1998   129.00 _____
____ Occupational Outlook Handbook, 1998-99   22.95 _____
____ O*NET Dictionary of Occupational Titles   49.95 _____
____ Professional Careers Sourcebook   99.00 _____
____ Specialty Occupational Outlook: Professions   49.95 _____
____ Specialty Occupational Outlook: Trade & Technical   49.95 _____
____ Vocational Careers Sourcebook   82.00 _____

Education Directories

____ Free and Inexpensive Career Materials   19.95 _____
____ Internships 1999   24.95 _____
____ Peterson's Guide to Graduate & Professional Programs 239.95 _____
____ Peterson's Two- and Four-Year Colleges 1999   45.95 _____
____ Scholarships, Fellowships, & Loans 1999   165.00 _____

Electronic Jobs Search

____ CareerXroads 1998   22.95 _____
____ Guide to Internet Job Search   14.95 _____
____ How to Get Your Dream Job Using the Web   29.99 _____

Best Companies

____ Hidden Job Market 1999   18.95 _____
____ Hoover's Top 2,500 Employers   22.95 _____

___	Job Vault	20.00	___
___	JobBank Guide to Computer & High-Tech Companies	16.95	___
___	JobBank Guide to Health Care Companies	16.95	___

$100,000+ Jobs

___	The $100,000 Club	25.00	___
___	100 Winning Resumes For $100,000+ Jobs	24.95	___
___	201 Winning Cover Letters For $100,000+ Jobs	24.95	___
___	1500+ KeyWords For $100,000+ Jobs	14.95	___
___	New Rites of Passage at $100,000+	29.95	___
___	Six-Figure Consulting	17.95	___

Finding Great Jobs

___	100 Best Careers in Casinos and Casino Hotels	15.95	___
___	101 Ways to Power Up Your Job Search	12.95	___
___	110 Biggest Mistakes Job Hunters Make	19.95	___
___	Alternative Careers in Secret Operations	19.95	___
___	Back Door Guide to Short-Term Job Adventures	19.95	___
___	Careers For College Majors	32.95	___
___	College Grad Job Hunter	14.95	___
___	Directory of Executive Recruiters 1998	44.95	___
___	Get Ahead! Stay Ahead!	12.95	___
___	Get a Job You Love!	19.95	___
___	Get What You Deserve!	23.00	___
___	Great Jobs For Liberal Arts Majors	11.95	___
___	In Transition	12.50	___
___	Job Hunting Made Easy	12.95	___
___	Job Search: The Total System	14.95	___
___	Job Search 101	12.95	___
___	Jobs & Careers With Nonprofit Organizations	15.95	___
___	Knock 'Em Dead	12.95	___
___	New Relocating Spouse's Guide to Employment	14.95	___
___	No One Is Unemployable	29.95	___
___	Non-Profits and Education Job Finder	16.95	___
___	Perfect Pitch	13.99	___
___	Professional's Job Finder	18.95	___
___	Strategic Job Jumping	20.00	___
___	Top Career Strategies For the Year 2000 & Beyond	12.00	___
___	What Do I Say Next?	20.00	___
___	What Employers Really Want.	14.95	___
___	Work Happy Live Healthy	14.95	___
___	You Can't Play the Game If You Don't Know the Rules	14.95	___

Assessment

___	Discover the Best Jobs For You	14.95	___
___	Discover What You're Best At	12.00	___
___	Do What You Are	16.95	___
___	Finding Your Perfect Work	16.95	___
___	I Could Do Anything If Only I Knew What It Was	19.95	___

Inspiration & Empowerment

___	100 Ways to Motivate Yourself	15.99	___
___	Chicken Soup For the Soul Series	75.95	___

___	Doing Work You Love	14.95 ___
___	Emotional Intelligence	13.95 ___
___	Personal Job Power	12.95 ___
___	Power of Purpose	20.00 ___
___	Seven Habits of Highly Effective People	14.00 ___
___	Survival Personality	12.00 ___
___	Your Signature Path	24.95 ___

Resumes

___	100 Winning Resumes For $100,000+ Jobs	24.95 ___
___	101 Best Resumes	10.95 ___
___	101 Quick Tips For a Dynamite Resume	13.95 ___
___	1500+ KeyWords For $100,000+ Jobs	14.95 ___
___	Adams Resumes Almanac & Disk	19.95 ___
___	America's Top Resumes For America's Top Jobs	19.95 ___
___	Asher's Bible of Executive Resumes	29.95 ___
___	Better Resumes in Three Easy Steps	12.95 ___
___	Complete Idiot's Guide to Writing the Perfect Resume	16.95 ___
___	Designing the Perfect Resume	12.95 ___
___	Dynamite Resumes	14.95 ___
___	Encyclopedia of Job-Winning Resumes	16.95 ___
___	Gallery of Best Resumes	16.95 ___
___	Heart and Soul Resumes	15.95 ___
___	High Impact Resumes & Letters	19.95 ___
___	Internet Resumes	14.95 ___
___	New 90-Minute Resumes	15.95 ___
___	New Perfect Resume	12.00 ___
___	Portfolio Power	14.95 ___
___	Ready-to-Go Resumes	29.95 ___
___	Resume Catalog	15.95 ___
___	Resume Shortcuts	14.95 ___
___	Resumes & Job Search Letters For Transitioning Military Personnel	17.95 ___
___	Resumes For Dummies	12.99 ___
___	Resumes For Re-Entry	10.95 ___
___	Resumes in Cyberspace	14.95 ___
___	Resumes That Knock 'Em Dead	14.95 ___
___	Sure-Hire Resumes	14.95 ___

Cover Letters

___	175 High-Impact Cover Letters	10.95 ___
___	201 Dynamite Job Search Letters	19.95 ___
___	201 Killer Cover Letters	16.95 ___
___	201 Winning Cover Letters For $100,000+ Jobs	24.95 ___
___	Complete Idiot's Guide to the Perfect Cover Letter	14.95 ___
___	Cover Letters For Dummies	12.99 ___
___	Cover Letters That Knock 'Em Dead	10.95 ___
___	Dynamite Cover Letters	14.95 ___

Networking

___	Dynamite Networking For Dynamite Jobs	15.95 ___
___	Dynamite Telesearch	12.95 ___
___	Great Connections	19.95 ___
___	How to Work a Room	11.99 ___

___	People Power	14.95	___
___	Power Networking	14.95	___
___	Power Schmoozing	12.95	___
___	Power to Get In	24.95	___

Interview & Communication Skills

___	90-Minute Interview Prep Book	15.95	___
___	101 Dynamite Answers to Interview Questions	12.95	___
___	101 Dynamite Questions to Ask At Your Job Interview	14.95	___
___	101 Secrets of Highly Effective Speakers	14.95	___
___	111 Dynamite Ways to Ace Your Job Interview	13.95	___
___	Complete Idiot's Guide to the Perfect Job Interview	14.95	___
___	Complete Q & A Job Interview Book	14.95	___
___	Interview For Success	15.95	___
___	Job Interview For Dummies	12.99	___

Salary Negotiations

___	Dynamite Salary Negotiations	15.95	___
___	Get a Raise in 7 Days	14.95	___
___	Get More Money On Your Next Job	14.95	___
___	Negotiate Your Job Offer	14.95	___

SUBTOTAL ___

Virginia residents add 4½% sales tax ___

POSTAGE/HANDLING ($5 for first
product and 8% of SUBTOTAL over $30) $5.00

8% of SUBTOTAL over $30 -------------------------- ___

TOTAL ENCLOSED ------------------------- ___

NAME _____

ADDRESS _____

_____

_____

❑ I enclose check/moneyorder for $ _____ made payable to
IMPACT PUBLICATIONS.

❑ Please charge $ _____ to my credit card:
❑ Visa ❑ MasterCard ❑ American Express ❑ Discover

Card # _____

Expiration date: ____/____ Phone _____

Signature _____

Your One-Stop Online Superstore
Hundreds of Terrific Resources Conveniently Available On the World Wide Web 24-Hours a Day, 365 Days a Year!

Ever wanted to know what are the newest and best books, directories, newsletters, wall charts, training programs, videos, CD-ROMs, computer software, and kits available to help you land a job, negotiate a higher salary, or start your own business? What about finding a job in Asia or relocating to San Francisco? Are you curious about how to find a job 24-hours a day by using the Internet or what you'll be doing five years from now? Trying to keep up-to-date on the latest career resources but not able to find the latest catalogs, brochures, or newsletters on today's "best of the best" resources?

Welcome to the first virtual career bookstore on the Internet. Now you're only a "click" away with Impact Publication's electronic solution to the resource challenge. Impact Publications, one of the nation's leading publishers and distributors of career resources, offers the most comprehensive "Career Superstore and Warehouse" on the Internet. The bookstore is jam-packed with the latest job and career resources on:

- Alternative jobs and careers
- Self-assessment
- Career planning and job search
- Employers
- Relocation and cities
- Resumes
- Cover Letters
- Dress, image, and etiquette
- Education
- Recruitment
- Military
- Salaries
- Interviewing
- Nonprofits
- Empowerment
- Self-esteem
- Goal setting
- Executive recruiters
- Entrepreneurship
- Government
- Networking
- Electronic job search
- International jobs
- Travel
- Law
- Training and presentations
- Minorities
- Physically challenged

The bookstore also includes sections for ex-offenders and middle schools.

"This is more than just a bookstore offering lots of product," say Drs. Ron and Caryl Krannich, two of the nation's leading career experts and authors and developers of this on-line bookstore. *"We're an important resource center for libraries, corporations, government, educators, trainers, and career counselors who are constantly defining and redefining this dynamic field. Of the thousands of career resources we review each year, we only select the 'best of the best.'"*

Visit this rich site and you'll quickly discover just about everything you ever wanted to know about finding jobs, changing careers, and starting your own business—including many useful resources that are difficult to find in local bookstores and libraries. The site also includes tips for job search success and monthly specials. Its shopping cart and special search feature make this one of the most convenient Web sites to use. Impact's Internet address is:

www.impactpublications.com